UNDERSTANDING THE MINDS OF BUYERS

I n the bustling marketplace of the 21st century, the behavior of consumers is an intricate and ever-evolving phenomenon that continues to intrigue marketers, researchers, and businesses alike. Understanding why consumers make the choices they do, how they perceive products and brands, and what factors influence their decision-making processes is at the heart of consumer psychology. This multifaceted field examines the intricacies of human behavior, cognition, and emotion as they relate to the act of consumption. It seeks to unravel the mysteries behind why individuals purchase certain products, form brand loyalties, and respond to marketing strategies in specific ways.

Consumer psychology is more than just a mere curiosity; it is an indispensable tool for businesses striving to thrive in the fiercely competitive global marketplace. By comprehending the psychological underpinnings of consumer behavior, companies can tailor their products, marketing campaigns, and customer experiences to meet the unique needs and desires of their target audience. This, in turn, can lead to increased sales, brand loyalty, and long-term business success. This introduction aims to provide an in-depth exploration of consumer psychology, its history, fundamental concepts, and its critical role in shaping the contemporary world of commerce.

Consumer psychology as a distinct field of study has its roots in the early 20th century, when businesses began to recognize the importance of understanding customer behavior. The industrial revolution had transformed the marketplace, leading to the mass production of goods and an explosion of advertising. With this shift came a need for businesses to gain insights into consumer preferences, motivations, and decision-making processes.

One of the seminal figures in the development of consumer psychology was Walter Dill Scott, an American psychologist who, in the early 1900s, conducted pioneering research on advertising and consumer behavior. His work laid the foundation for the application of psychological principles in marketing and advertising. Around the same time, John B. Watson, often considered the father of behaviorism, emphasized the importance of studying observable behaviors and their underlying causes, a perspective that significantly influenced consumer psychology.

Over the decades, consumer psychology continued to evolve, integrating insights from fields such as cognitive psychology, social psychology, and neuroscience. As technological advancements provided new tools for data collection and analysis, researchers gained a deeper understanding of the cognitive processes, emotional responses, and social influences that drive consumer behavior. Today, consumer psychology is a well-established and interdisciplinary field that informs marketing strategies, product design, and business decision-making.

Consumer psychology is built upon a set of fundamental concepts that shed light on the complex interplay between individuals and the marketplace. These concepts serve as a roadmap for understanding consumer behavior and developing effective marketing strategies.

One of the cornerstones of consumer psychology is the study of perception. How consumers perceive products, brands, and marketing messages greatly influences their purchasing decisions. Perceptual processes, such as attention, interpretation, and memory, shape how individuals make sense of their environment and evaluate the desirability of products. For example, a well-designed logo can capture a consumer's attention and create a favorable impression of a brand, while a confusing label may lead to product rejection.

Consumer behavior is driven by a complex interplay of motivations and needs. Maslow's hierarchy of needs, for instance, suggests that individuals have a hierarchy of needs, ranging from physiological needs (e.g., food and shelter) to self-actualization needs (e.g., personal growth and fulfillment). Understanding which needs a product fulfills and how it aligns with consumers' motivations is essential for effective marketing.

Consumers bring a set of attitudes and beliefs to the marketplace that influence their preferences and choices. These attitudes and beliefs are often shaped by cultural, social, and personal factors. Marketers seek to understand and, when possible, influence these attitudes through advertising, branding, and messaging.

Consumer decisions are rarely made in isolation; instead, they follow a series of stages. This decision-making process can be divided into several phases, including problem recognition, information search, evaluation of alternatives, purchase, and post-purchase evaluation. Businesses must tailor their marketing efforts to address consumers' needs and concerns at each of these stages.

Consumers are not isolated entities but are deeply embedded in social and cultural contexts. Social influences, such as peer pressure and social norms, play a significant role in shaping consumer behavior. Additionally, culture exerts a profound impact on consumer preferences, as it influences values, traditions, and symbols that guide consumption choices.

Emotions are a powerful force in consumer psychology. They can shape preferences, influence purchasing decisions, and drive brand loyalty. Understanding the emotional aspects of consumer behavior is crucial for businesses aiming to create meaningful connections with their customers.

Emotions often serve as a bridge between rational decision-making and impulsive buying. For example, a consumer may choose a particular brand of chocolate not solely based on its taste and price but also because it evokes positive feelings and nostalgia. Similarly, luxury brands often leverage emotions such as prestige and exclusivity to attract consumers willing to pay a premium for their products.

Emotions can impact post-purchase behavior, including customer satisfaction and loyalty. A positive emotional experience during a purchase can lead to repeat business and word-of-mouth recommendations. Conversely, a negative emotional experience can result in customer churn and reputational damage.

Marketers employ various strategies to evoke specific emotions in consumers. This can involve using storytelling in advertising, employing color psychology in branding, or creating immersive retail environments that trigger positive emotional responses. Understanding the emotional triggers that resonate with their target audience allows businesses to craft more effective marketing campaigns and foster deeper connections with consumers.

The advent of the digital age has revolutionized consumer behavior and reshaped the way businesses interact with their customers. The internet, social media, e-commerce platforms, and mobile devices have not only expanded the avenues through which consumers access products and information but have also generated vast amounts of data that provide insights into consumer behavior.

Online shopping has transformed the retail landscape. Consumers can now browse, compare, and purchase products from the comfort of their homes or on-the-go. This shift has given rise to new challenges and opportunities for businesses. They must optimize their online presence, provide seamless user experiences, and utilize data analytics to understand and anticipate consumer preferences.

Social media platforms have become influential in shaping consumer opinions and trends. Consumers share their experiences, reviews, and recommendations, which can go viral and impact brand perception. Social media also allows businesses to engage with their audience directly, fostering brand loyalty and providing opportunities for targeted advertising.

The abundance of data generated by digital interactions has enabled businesses to personalize their marketing efforts. Through the use of algorithms and machine learning, companies can tailor product recommendations, advertisements, and content to individual preferences. This level of personalization has the potential to enhance the customer experience and drive sales.

The digital realm also raises concerns about privacy and data security. Consumers are increasingly aware of the data they share and expect businesses to handle their information responsibly. Balancing the benefits of data-driven marketing with ethical considerations is a complex challenge that businesses must navigate in the digital age.

Consumer psychology is not merely an academic pursuit; it is a practical and strategic tool for businesses seeking to thrive in the competitive marketplace. Here, we look into how consumer psychology is applied in real-world marketing and business strategies.

Understanding the diversity of consumer preferences is a fundamental principle of consumer psychology. Businesses segment their target market into distinct groups based on demographics, psychographics, and behavioral traits. By tailoring products and marketing messages to specific segments, companies can increase the relevance of their offerings and connect more effectively with consumers. For example, a sportswear company may create different product lines and marketing campaigns for fitness enthusiasts, professional athletes, and casual gym-goers, recognizing that each group has unique needs and motivations.

Branding is a powerful psychological tool that can influence consumer perceptions and choices. The process of branding involves creating a distinct identity and personality for a product or company. Successful brands evoke emotional connections with consumers, fostering trust, loyalty, and even advocacy. Consumer psychology guides businesses in crafting brand images that resonate with their target audience. For example, luxury brands often use exclusivity and prestige to create a sense of aspiration and desire among consumers.

Consumer psychology plays a pivotal role in the development of advertising strategies. Advertisements are designed to grab consumers' attention, elicit emotions, and persuade them to take action, whether it's making a purchase or signing up for a newsletter. Techniques such as storytelling, social proof, and the use of persuasive language are informed by psychological principles. For instance, testimonials from satisfied customers can build trust, and scarcity tactics, like "limited-time offers," can create a sense of urgency.

Pricing is a complex and highly psychological aspect of consumer behavior. Consumers often perceive value not only in terms of the actual price but also in relation to the perceived quality of a product or service. Businesses employ various pricing strategies, such as discounts, bundling, and psychological pricing (e.g., pricing products at $9.99 instead of $10), to influence consumer perceptions and behavior.

Moreover, dynamic pricing, made possible by data analytics, allows companies to adjust prices in real-time based on consumer demand and competitor pricing.

The consumer journey extends beyond the purchase itself to encompass the entire customer experience. Consumer psychology informs businesses on how to create positive experiences at every touchpoint, from website design and customer service interactions to product packaging and post-purchase follow-ups. Exceptional customer experiences can lead to customer satisfaction, repeat business, and word-of-mouth referrals.

In today's socially conscious consumer landscape, ethical considerations play a significant role. Businesses must align their practices with consumer values, which can include sustainability, transparency, and social responsibility. Understanding consumer psychology helps companies navigate these concerns by building trust and demonstrating their commitment to ethical principles.

Consumer psychology relies on a robust theoretical framework to illuminate the intricate processes at play in the consumer mind. These theories provide valuable insights into the mechanisms that drive consumer behavior:

The Theory of Planned Behavior (TPB): This influential theory posits that consumers' intentions and behaviors are influenced by three key factors: their attitudes toward a product or service, the subjective norms surrounding it, and their perceived behavioral control. Understanding these factors allows marketers to tailor their strategies accordingly.

The Elaboration Likelihood Model (ELM): ELM suggests that consumers process information in two distinct ways: central and peripheral routes. The central route involves careful consideration and evaluation of information, while the peripheral route relies on heuristics and cues. Recognizing which route consumers are likely to take helps marketers craft persuasive messages.

Motivation-Need Theory: Rooted in psychology, this theory posits that consumers have different motivations and needs, which drive their purchasing decisions. Abraham Maslow's Hierarchy of Needs is a famous example, categorizing needs from basic physiological ones to higher-level self-actualization needs.

Consumer psychology's significance extends well beyond the realm of academia. It is an indispensable tool for businesses and marketers, offering insights that can make or break a company's success in the marketplace. Here's how consumer psychology is intrinsically linked to marketing:

Understanding Consumer Motivation: Consumer psychology helps marketers investigate into the underlying motivations and desires that lead consumers to seek out specific products or services. By understanding these motivations, marketers can craft messages and campaigns that resonate with their target audience.

Building Emotional Connections: Emotional responses play a pivotal role in consumer decision-making. Leveraging insights from consumer psychology, marketers can create emotionally compelling advertisements and branding that forge deep connections with consumers, leading to brand loyalty and advocacy.

Leveraging Behavioral Economics: Consumer psychology has given rise to the field of behavioral economics, which examines how psychological factors influence economic decisions. Concepts like loss aversion, scarcity, and anchoring are frequently used by marketers to influence consumer choices and behaviors.

Segmentation and Personalization: Not all consumers are the same, and consumer psychology provides the foundation for segmenting target audiences based on their diverse needs and preferences. Marketers can then tailor their messaging and offerings to each segment, increasing the relevance

Consumer psychology is a captivating and indispensable field that unravels the intricacies of human behavior in the marketplace. Its historical evolution, fundamental concepts, and practical applications have illuminated the path for businesses to understand and connect with consumers in profound ways. In an era defined by rapid technological advancements and shifting consumer expectations, the role of consumer psychology has never been more critical.

As businesses continue to adapt to the dynamic landscape of commerce, they must remain committed to understanding the ever-evolving desires, motivations, and perceptions of their customers. By leveraging the insights gained from consumer psychology, companies can craft marketing strategies, develop products, and provide experiences that resonate with consumers on a profound level. In doing so, they can foster brand loyalty, increase sales, and ultimately thrive in the competitive global marketplace. Consumer psychology is not merely a subject of academic interest; it is a guiding light that illuminates the path to business success in the modern world.

The Role of Trust in Consumer Decision-Making

Trust is a fundamental element in the world of consumer decision-making. In an era where consumers are bombarded with choices and information, trust serves as the linchpin that guides their choices. Whether it's selecting a product, a service provider, or an e-commerce platform, consumers place immense importance on trust. In this section, we will traverse into the multifaceted role of trust in consumer decision-making, exploring its various dimensions, the factors that influence it, and its profound impact on brand loyalty and purchasing behavior.

A critical aspect of trust in consumer decision-making is brand reputation. Consumers often rely on a brand's reputation as a shortcut for evaluating product or service quality. Brands that have consistently delivered on their promises and maintained a positive image over time tend to enjoy a higher level of trust among consumers.

Reputation is built through a combination of factors:

Consistency: Consistently delivering quality products or services and maintaining a consistent brand identity over time fosters trust. Consumers know what to expect.

Transparency: Brands that are transparent about their business practices, pricing, and product information are seen as more trustworthy. Transparency creates a perception of honesty and integrity.

Customer Reviews and Testimonials: Positive customer reviews and testimonials serve as social proof of a brand's trustworthiness. Consumers are more likely to trust the experiences of their peers.

Ethical Practices: Brands that demonstrate ethical behavior, such as fair labor practices, sustainability efforts, and responsible sourcing, can build trust by aligning with consumer values.

Crisis Management: How a brand handles crises or setbacks can significantly impact trust. Swift, transparent, and responsible responses can help mitigate damage to trust.

Trust in a brand's reputation serves as a foundation upon which consumers base their initial consideration of a product or service.

Consumers have access to an abundance of information, but not all sources are considered trustworthy. The role of trust extends to the sources from which consumers gather information about products or services. These sources include:

Word of Mouth: Recommendations from friends, family, or acquaintances hold significant weight in consumer decisions. Trust in these sources is grounded in personal relationships and shared experiences.

Online Reviews and Ratings: Consumer-generated online reviews and ratings on platforms like Amazon, Yelp, and TripAdvisor play a crucial role in trust formation. Consumers trust the opinions of fellow shoppers who have firsthand experience with a product or service.

Expert Opinions: Experts in various fields, such as product reviewers, influencers, and industry professionals, can influence consumer decisions. Trust in experts is based on their knowledge and credibility.

Brand Websites and Content: Consumers often visit a brand's official website for information. Trust is established when the website is well-designed, informative, and user-friendly.

Content that educates, informs, and addresses consumer concerns builds trust.

Social Media: Brands that maintain a strong and authentic presence on social media platforms can earn the trust of consumers. Consistent, engaging, and responsive social media interactions contribute to trust formation.

Trust in these information sources helps consumers navigate the overwhelming amount of information available, guiding them toward making informed decisions.

Trust is not solely a rational or cognitive process; it also has deep emotional dimensions. Emotional engagement is a crucial component of trust, and consumers often rely on their feelings and intuitions when making decisions.

Brand Storytelling: Brands that tell compelling stories that resonate with consumers' emotions can establish a deep connection. Stories that evoke empathy, joy, nostalgia, or inspiration create positive emotional associations.

Consistency of Experience: When consumers consistently have positive experiences with a brand, they develop an emotional attachment. These positive emotions create trust and loyalty.

Customer Service: Exceptional customer service, characterized by empathy, responsiveness, and problem-solving, can generate trust and foster emotional engagement.

Alignment with Values: Brands that align with consumers' personal values and beliefs create an emotional connection. Consumers trust brands that share their convictions.

Surprise and Delight: Unexpected gestures of appreciation, such as personalized notes, discounts, or gifts, can trigger positive emotions and strengthen trust.

Emotional engagement contributes to brand loyalty, as consumers are more likely to choose brands that make them feel a sense of belonging, happiness, or fulfillment.

Trust plays a pivotal role in the context of online transactions, where consumers often make purchases from distant and unfamiliar entities. Several trust-related factors influence online consumer behavior:

Website Security: Trust is closely tied to the perception of a secure online environment. Consumers look for visual cues such as secure payment gateways, SSL certificates, and trust badges.

Privacy and Data Security: Trust in online transactions is contingent on the assurance that personal and financial information will be handled securely and responsibly.

Return and Refund Policies: Clear, fair, and flexible return and refund policies enhance trust by reducing perceived risk.

User Reviews and Ratings: Online shoppers rely on the experiences of others as a trust-building mechanism. Brands with a history of positive reviews and ratings are more likely to be trusted.

Trust Symbols: Recognizable trust symbols and logos, such as the Better Business Bureau (BBB) seal or PayPal's secure payment logo, can instill confidence in consumers.

Trust in online transactions is essential for converting website visitors into customers. Businesses that prioritize online trust-building measures can increase their conversion rates and long-term customer loyalty.

Trust is not static; it can be challenged or broken due to various factors, including product defects, poor customer service, or breaches of trust. However, the way a brand responds to trust challenges can have a profound impact on customer loyalty.

Trust recovery involves acknowledging mistakes, taking responsibility, and making amends. When a brand effectively addresses trust breaches, it can actually enhance trust and loyalty. Trust recovery strategies include:

Apology and Transparency: Acknowledging the issue and

providing a sincere apology can rebuild trust. Transparency about the cause and steps taken to prevent future issues is crucial.

Compensation or Restitution: Offering compensation, such as refunds, replacements, or discounts, can demonstrate commitment to customer satisfaction and trust restoration.

Improved Processes: Taking concrete steps to prevent future trust breaches, such as implementing quality control measures or enhancing customer service training, shows a commitment to improvement.

Engagement and Communication: Consistent communication with affected customers and follow-up to ensure their needs are met can rebuild trust and retain loyalty.

Trust recovery demonstrates a brand's commitment to its customers and its willingness to learn from mistakes, ultimately strengthening customer loyalty.

Trust is a foundational element in consumer decision-making, influencing brand reputation, information sources, emotional engagement, online transactions, and loyalty. Businesses that understand the multifaceted role of trust and invest in trust-building measures can foster deeper connections with customers, enhance brand loyalty, and gain a competitive edge in a crowded marketplace.

Trust is not merely a transactional concept; it is a long-term relationship that requires ongoing nurturing and maintenance. Brands that consistently deliver on promises, prioritize transparency, and respond effectively to trust challenges are more likely to earn and retain the trust of their customers. In conclusion, trust is not just a factor in consumer decision-making; it is the glue that binds customers to brands. Businesses that recognize the importance of trust and prioritize its cultivation and maintenance are better positioned to thrive in an environment where consumers demand not only quality products and services but also integrity, reliability, and emotional connection. Trust is not built overnight, but by consistently demonstrating honesty, reliability, and a commitment to customer satisfaction, businesses can forge lasting relationships with their customers, leading to loyalty and long-term success.

The Psychology of Logos
and Symbols

L ogos and symbols are integral components of brand identity and communication. In the realm of consumer psychology, these visual elements wield immense influence. They have the power to shape perceptions, evoke emotions, and establish strong connections with consumers. In this section, we will embark into the psychology of logos and symbols for the consumer, exploring how these visual cues can impact consumer behavior, drive brand loyalty, and convey messages far beyond words.

Humans are inherently visual beings, with a significant portion of the brain dedicated to processing visual information. This predisposition toward visual stimuli makes logos and symbols highly effective tools for communicating with consumers. They serve as shortcuts to convey complex ideas and emotions, often in a split second.

Logos, in particular, encapsulate a brand's essence and values in a single, memorable image. For instance, the bitten apple of Apple Inc. symbolizes innovation and the "think different" ethos. The iconic Nike swoosh represents athleticism, action, and achievement. These symbols create instant recognition, eliciting positive associations and emotions in consumers.

Color is a fundamental aspect of logos and symbols, and it plays a significant role in shaping consumer perceptions and emotions. Color psychology is the study of how different colors evoke specific emotional responses. Brands strategically leverage this knowledge to elicit desired feelings and associations through their logos and symbols.

The red used in the Coca-Cola logo stimulates excitement and energy, while the blue in the Facebook logo conveys trust and reliability. The green in the Starbucks logo represents freshness and sustainability, appealing to environmentally conscious consumers. These color choices are not arbitrary; they are carefully selected to align with the brand's identity and the emotions it seeks to evoke in consumers.

Logos and symbols are rich in symbolism, often drawing on cultural, historical, or mythological references to convey deeper meanings. The use of symbolism allows brands to tap into shared cultural narratives and resonate with consumers on a profound level.

Consider the Starbucks logo, which features a siren from Greek mythology. This symbolizes seduction, allure, and the irresistible draw of the brand's coffee. Similarly, the Mercedes-Benz logo, a three-pointed star, represents the brand's dominance in land, sea, and air transportation.

Cultural sensitivity is essential when incorporating symbolism into logos and symbols, as misinterpretation or insensitivity can lead to backlash and damage the brand's reputation.

Successful brands understand the need for logo evolution and adaptation to stay relevant in changing consumer landscapes. Over time, consumer preferences, design trends, and societal values shift. To maintain resonance with consumers, brands may update or refresh their logos and symbols.

The Pepsi logo has undergone multiple transformations, reflecting changing design aesthetics and consumer expectations. Each iteration maintains a connection to the brand's heritage while incorporating contemporary elements.

Adaptation is not limited to design aesthetics; it can also involve making logos more inclusive and representative. In recent years, many brands have reimagined their logos to be more diverse and inclusive, reflecting changing societal norms and values.

The ultimate goal of logos and symbols in consumer psychology is to establish a deep emotional connection between the brand and its consumers. Emotions play a significant role in consumer decision-making, often driving brand loyalty and advocacy.

A well-designed logo or symbol can trigger positive emotions and create a sense of belonging. For example, the iconic Apple logo evokes feelings of innovation, elegance, and belonging to a community of Apple users.

An emotional connection with a brand can lead to higher customer retention rates and increased brand advocacy. Consumers who feel emotionally connected to a brand are more likely to forgive occasional missteps and continue supporting the brand through thick and thin.

Logos and symbols are potent tools in the arsenal of consumer psychology. They harness the brain's predisposition for visual processing, leverage color psychology, draw on symbolism, and facilitate emotional connections between consumers and brands. As consumers navigate a sea of choices in an increasingly visual world, logos and symbols provide a beacon of recognition and meaning. Understanding the psychology behind logos and symbols empowers businesses to craft visual identities that resonate deeply with consumers, foster brand loyalty, and convey their values and messages effectively.

The Psychology of Colors

The psychology of colors has long fascinated marketers, designers, and psychologists alike. Colors have a profound influence on our emotions, perceptions, and behaviors. When it comes to consumer experiences, understanding how different colors can affect the decisions people make is a powerful tool. In this section, we will explore into the psychology of colors for the consumer, exploring how various colors evoke specific emotions and why businesses should harness this knowledge to create impactful branding, marketing, and product design strategies.

Red: The Color of Passion and Urgency

Red is a color that exudes energy, passion, and excitement. It is often associated with strong emotions like love and anger. In the realm of consumer psychology, red is frequently used to create a sense of urgency and encourage impulsive buying decisions. Fast-food chains like McDonald's and KFC prominently use red in their branding to stimulate appetite and prompt quick purchases. Red can also convey a feeling of warmth and comfort. This is why it's used by brands like Coca-Cola, which wants consumers to associate its product with feelings of happiness and togetherness. However, it's essential to use red judiciously, as excessive exposure can be overwhelming or even agitating, depending on the context and audience.

Blue: The Color of Trust and Serenity

Blue is often regarded as one of the most universally liked colors, symbolizing trust, reliability, and calmness. In consumer psychology, blue is frequently employed by brands seeking to establish trust and authority in their respective industries. Companies like IBM, Facebook, and Ford incorporate blue into their logos and branding to convey a sense of stability and dependability. Blue is associated with serenity and relaxation, making it a popular choice for brands in the health and wellness industry. Hospitals, pharmaceutical companies, and meditation apps often use shades of blue to evoke feelings of tranquility and well-being in consumers.

Green: The Color of Health and Eco-Friendliness

Green is closely linked to nature, growth, and health. It represents freshness, renewal, and sustainability. In consumer psychology, green is employed to appeal to environmentally conscious individuals and promote eco-friendly products and practices. Brands like Whole Foods and The Body Shop use green to convey their commitment to health, organic products, and environmental responsibility. Green also signifies growth and abundance, making it a suitable choice for financial and wealth-related industries. Banks, investment firms, and financial apps utilize green to instill confidence in consumers regarding their financial stability and growth potential.

Yellow: The Color of Optimism and Attention

Yellow is a vibrant and attention-grabbing color associated with optimism, happiness, and energy. In consumer psychology, yellow is often used to capture attention and stimulate positive emotions. Brands like McDonald's use yellow to create a sense of happiness and friendliness in their fast-food establishments. Yellow is also known for enhancing clarity and memory retention, making it suitable for signage, call-to-action buttons, and warning labels. However, it's important to use yellow thoughtfully, as excessive use can lead to feelings of anxiety or impatience.

Black: The Color of Elegance and Luxury

Black is a color of sophistication, luxury, and timelessness. It exudes a sense of power and authority. In consumer psychology, black is frequently employed by high-end fashion brands, luxury car manufacturers, and upscale electronics companies to convey elegance and exclusivity. Brands like Chanel, Mercedes-Benz, and Apple utilize black to create a sense of prestige and desirability. While black is associated with luxury, it can also symbolize mystery and rebellion, making it an excellent choice for edgy and alternative brands that want to appeal to a more rebellious or unconventional audience.

The psychology of not using a red pen in business communication is rooted in cultural and psychological associations. In many Western cultures, the color red is commonly associated with errors, warnings, or negative feedback. When used to mark or edit documents, the red pen can evoke feelings of critique and judgment, potentially leading to defensiveness or resistance from the recipient. In business, where clear and effective communication is essential, professionals often opt for more neutral colors like black or blue to provide feedback or make corrections. This choice reflects an understanding of the psychological impact that colors can have on perception and how business communication aims to maintain a positive and constructive tone while avoiding unnecessary conflict or misunderstandings.

The psychology of colors plays a pivotal role in consumer decision-making, influencing emotions, perceptions, and behaviors. By understanding the psychological impact of colors, businesses can strategically design their branding, marketing materials, and product packaging to evoke desired emotions and connect with their target audience on a deeper level. Effective use of colors can not only capture attention but also build trust, convey value, and create memorable consumer experiences. As businesses continue to explore the psychology of colors, they unlock a potent tool for enhancing their brand identity and driving consumer engagement and loyalty.

The Psychology of Slogans

Slogans, also known as taglines or catchphrases, serve as concise and memorable expressions of a brand's identity and values. They are an essential component of marketing and communication strategies, designed to leave a lasting impression on consumers. Understanding the psychology behind slogans is crucial for businesses seeking to connect with their target audience, convey key messages, and build brand recognition. In this section, we will explore the psychology of slogans for the consumer, examining how these succinct phrases tap into emotions, influence decision-making, and create lasting brand associations.

Slogans have the power to evoke strong emotional responses in consumers. The words and phrases chosen in a slogan can trigger feelings of nostalgia, excitement, trust, or even humor. The emotional resonance that slogans create is a critical factor in shaping consumer perceptions and building brand identity.

Nike's famous slogan, "Just Do It," encapsulates a sense of determination, motivation, and empowerment. When consumers encounter this slogan, it triggers feelings of inspiration and encourages them to take action. This emotional connection not only reinforces the brand's identity as a catalyst for athletes but also fosters loyalty among those who share these values.

McDonald's iconic slogan, "I'm Lovin' It," invokes a sense of joy, comfort, and satisfaction. It reinforces the brand's image as a provider of enjoyable fast-food experiences. The emotional appeal of this slogan helps create a sense of attachment and fondness among consumers.

Slogans are often brief and to the point, which facilitates cognitive processing and message retention. Consumers are inundated with information daily, and slogans serve as mental shortcuts that help them quickly understand and remember a brand's message.

A well-crafted slogan conveys the essence of a brand's value proposition and differentiates it from competitors. For instance, Apple's "Think Different" slogan not only communicates the brand's commitment to innovation but also implies a departure from the status quo. This succinct message positions Apple as a company that challenges conventions and encourages creativity.

Message clarity is essential in making a slogan effective. When consumers encounter a clear and concise slogan, it eliminates ambiguity and makes it easier for them to connect with the brand's core message. In contrast, vague or overly complex slogans can lead to confusion and may not resonate as strongly with consumers.

Consistency is a key element of brand recognition and recall. Slogans play a vital role in reinforcing brand consistency by encapsulating the brand's core values and identity in a memorable phrase. This consistency helps consumers recognize the brand across various touchpoints and reinforces their loyalty.

Coca-Cola's timeless slogan, "Open Happiness," embodies the brand's core promise of delivering joy and refreshment. This consistent messaging reinforces consumers' emotional connection with the brand, ensuring that every encounter with Coca-Cola evokes feelings of happiness and satisfaction.

Brand recognition is further enhanced when slogans are integrated into other marketing elements, such as logo design, advertising campaigns, and social media content. When consumers see a slogan paired with the brand's visual identity, it triggers instant recognition and reinforces the brand's messaging.

Slogans are persuasive tools that can influence consumer behavior and decision-making. They are often used to encourage consumers to take specific actions, such as making a purchase, trying a new product, or supporting a cause.

Subway's slogan, "Eat Fresh," conveys a message of health and freshness. This slogan encourages consumers to choose Subway as a healthier alternative to traditional fast food. The persuasive power of this slogan lies in its ability to tap into consumers' desire for nutritious options.

Slogans can also be used to instill a sense of urgency or FOMO (Fear of Missing Out). Phrases like "Limited Time Offer" or "Act Now" create a sense of urgency that can drive consumers to make immediate decisions.

Slogans can evoke a sense of belonging and identity. Brands often use slogans to create a sense of community among consumers who share common values or interests. For example, Apple's "Designed by Apple in California" slogan emphasizes the brand's commitment to innovation and craftsmanship, appealing to consumers who value design excellence.

While slogans can be powerful tools for communication, they must be adapted to different cultural contexts to avoid misinterpretation or cultural insensitivity. What works in one culture may not resonate in another, and slogans should be carefully crafted to align with local values and preferences.

When Kentucky Fried Chicken expanded into China, the slogan "Finger Lickin' Good" was translated to "Eat Your Fingers Off." This adaptation ensured that the message remained appealing and culturally appropriate to Chinese consumers.

Cultural sensitivity is crucial not only in translation but also in the choice of words and phrases. Slogans should avoid any potential cultural taboos or offensive language. Brands that navigate cultural nuances effectively can build stronger connections with consumers in diverse markets.

Slogans are potent tools that leverage psychology to create emotional connections, convey messages, and influence consumer behavior. They tap into emotions, facilitate message clarity, reinforce brand identity, and persuade consumers to take action. Effective slogans are a cornerstone of successful marketing and branding strategies, enabling businesses to establish lasting brand associations and build loyal customer relationships. By understanding the psychology of slogans and their impact on consumers, businesses can craft memorable and influential brand messages that resonate across cultures and generations.

The Psychology of a Jingle

A jingle is more than just a catchy tune; it's a powerful psychological tool that wields considerable influence over consumer behavior, brand recognition, and memory retention. These brief musical compositions, often accompanied by a memorable slogan, have the remarkable ability to embed themselves in our minds and shape our perceptions of products and brands. In this section we embark on a melodious exploration into the psychology of a jingle, uncovering how these simple sonic elements tap into our cognitive and emotional faculties, leaving a lasting imprint on consumer consciousness.

At the heart of any effective jingle is its catchiness, a quality rooted in the psychology of human perception and memory. Catchiness refers to a melody or rhythm that is easy to remember, repetitive, and inherently pleasing to the ear. It often involves simple, memorable lyrics that are easy to sing along with. The human brain is wired to respond positively to repetition and predictability in music, making catchy jingles incredibly effective.

From an evolutionary standpoint, our brains have evolved to recognize patterns and repetitions in sound, which could have been advantageous for survival. When a jingle's melody or rhythm aligns with this innate pattern-recognition mechanism, it becomes earworm material—a tune that burrows deep into our memory, often playing on a loop long after we've heard it. This memorability is a key driver of brand recognition and recall.

Jingles also have the capacity to evoke powerful emotions, a psychological mechanism that strengthens their impact on consumers. Music, in general, has a direct connection to our emotions, and jingles are no exception. When a jingle is designed to elicit specific emotional responses, it becomes a formidable tool for marketers.

A jingle with a cheerful, upbeat melody can create a sense of happiness and positivity, associating those emotions with a particular brand or product. Conversely, a jingle with a more somber or sentimental tone can evoke feelings of nostalgia or empathy. By tapping into these emotional responses, jingles forge deeper connections between consumers and brands, enhancing brand loyalty and trust.

The mnemonic power of jingles is a crucial aspect of their psychology. Mnemonics are memory aids that help us remember information more easily. Jingles act as sonic mnemonics, providing a simple and memorable way for consumers to recall a brand, product, or slogan. The combination of music and lyrics creates a mental anchor that facilitates memory retention.

A well-crafted jingle ensures that the brand or product name is not easily forgotten. The auditory cues provided by the jingle—whether it's a distinctive melody, rhyme, or rhythm —make it easier for consumers to retrieve the associated information from their memory when needed. This mnemonic reinforcement strengthens brand identity and makes it more likely for consumers to choose a familiar brand over competitors.

Jingles are also potent persuaders, subtly influencing consumer behavior and purchase decisions. They serve as a form of psychological priming, where exposure to a jingle can influence subsequent actions or choices. For example, hearing a jingle associated with a fast-food restaurant while driving can subconsciously prime a person to consider visiting that restaurant for their next meal.

The psychology behind this phenomenon lies in classical conditioning, a theory proposed by Ivan Pavlov. When a jingle consistently accompanies positive experiences or emotions related to a brand or product, consumers begin to associate those positive feelings with the brand. Over time, this conditioning can lead to increased brand loyalty and a higher likelihood of choosing that brand when making purchasing decisions.

While jingles are undeniably effective psychological tools, they also come with ethical considerations. Businesses must use jingles responsibly, ensuring that they do not exploit psychological mechanisms to manipulate or deceive consumers. Honesty and transparency in advertising and branding are paramount.

Businesses must consider the cultural and social contexts in which their jingles will be heard. What may be catchy and appropriate in one culture could be misunderstood or offensive in another. Cultural sensitivity and inclusivity are crucial when employing jingles in marketing campaigns.

In the realm of marketing and advertising, the psychology of a jingle is a symphony of catchiness, emotional resonance, mnemonic magic, subtle persuasion, and ethical considerations. Jingles have the remarkable ability to create lasting brand impressions, evoke emotions, enhance memory retention, and influence consumer behavior. When crafted with care and thoughtfulness, jingles can become enduring sonic signatures that shape the way consumers perceive and interact with products and brands. In the ever-evolving landscape of advertising, these melodious creations continue to be a powerful tool for businesses seeking to establish strong brand identities and foster connections with their audiences.

The Psychology of Smell

In the realm of consumer psychology, the power of the senses plays a profound role in shaping perceptions, emotions, and behaviors. Among the five senses, the sense of smell, often underestimated, has a remarkable capacity to influence consumer choices and experiences. This section embarks on a fragrant journey into the psychology of smell for the consumer, unraveling the intricate ways in which scents affect mood, memory, and decision-making. From the aroma of fresh-baked bread in a bakery to the subtle fragrance of a luxury perfume, understanding the psychology of smell is a key to creating memorable and enticing consumer experiences.

Olfactory memory, the ability to recall scents and the emotions associated with them, is a fundamental aspect of the psychology of smell. Unlike visual or auditory memories, which fade over time, scent memories can remain remarkably vivid for years, even decades. The olfactory system is intricately connected to the brain's limbic system, which is responsible for emotions and memory. This connection allows scents to evoke powerful emotional responses and trigger memories, often subconsciously.

In the realm of consumer behavior, olfactory memory plays a crucial role in brand recognition and loyalty. Businesses can create unique and memorable brand identities by associating their products or environments with distinctive scents. For example, the scent of a particular cologne may remind consumers of a cherished moment, making them more likely to repurchase. Harnessing the primacy of olfactory memory is a strategic tool for businesses looking to create lasting impressions.

Scent marketing, also known as aroma marketing or sensory marketing, is a burgeoning field that capitalizes on the psychology of smell to influence consumer behavior. Businesses, from retail stores to hotels and airlines, employ scent marketing to enhance the customer experience, create emotional connections, and increase sales.

Studies have shown that the smell of lavender can induce a sense of relaxation and reduce stress, making it a popular choice in spas and wellness centers. In retail, the scent of freshly baked goods can stimulate hunger and encourage customers to purchase food items. By strategically diffusing scents in their environments, businesses can create more appealing and enticing spaces that encourage consumers to linger, explore, and ultimately make purchases.

Scents have a direct and immediate impact on emotions, making them a potent tool for influencing consumer moods. Different scents can elicit a wide range of emotions, from comfort and nostalgia to excitement and relaxation. For example, the scent of pine needles may evoke memories of holiday celebrations, while the aroma of citrus can create a feeling of freshness and energy.

Businesses use the emotional power of scents to set the mood and ambiance in their establishments. In a retail store, the right scent can create a welcoming and positive atmosphere that encourages shoppers to stay longer and feel more comfortable. In the hospitality industry, hotels use scents to create a sense of luxury and relaxation in their lobbies and rooms. By aligning scents with desired emotional responses, businesses can enhance the overall consumer experience.

The psychology of smell also extends to consumer decision-making. Research has shown that scents can influence product preferences and choices. In a retail setting, for example, the scent of a particular fragrance may lead consumers to choose one brand of perfume over another. Similarly, the smell of freshly brewed coffee in a café can prompt customers to order a cup, even if they hadn't initially planned to do so.

Scent can also influence perceived product quality. Consumers often associate pleasant scents with higher quality products. For example, a store that smells of fresh leather may lead customers to perceive the merchandise as premium and well-crafted. Businesses can strategically use scent to enhance the perceived value of their products and influence purchase decisions.

While scent marketing can be a powerful tool, businesses must also consider ethical considerations and individual variations in scent preferences. Scents can be highly subjective, and what is pleasing to one person may be unpleasant to another. Using scents in public spaces, such as stores or hotels, should be done with sensitivity to individuals who may have allergies or sensitivities.

Transparency in scent marketing is essential. Businesses should inform customers when scents are used in their environments and provide options for those who may wish to avoid exposure. Ethical scent marketing practices ensure that consumers have a positive and respectful experience.

The psychology of smell for the consumer is a fascinating and often underestimated aspect of consumer behavior. Scents have the power to evoke memories, influence emotions, and shape consumer choices. By understanding the intricacies of olfactory memory, scent marketing, emotional responses to scents, and their impact on decision-making, businesses can harness the power of smell to create memorable and engaging consumer experiences. However, it is essential for businesses to use scent marketing ethically and with sensitivity to individual variations, ensuring that consumers have positive and respectful interactions with their brand. In the ever-evolving world of consumer psychology, the sense of smell remains a fragrant avenue for businesses to connect with their customers on a deeper and more emotional level.

The Psychology of Music

Music, a universal language that transcends borders and cultures, holds a unique power to influence human emotions and behaviors. In the realm of consumer psychology, understanding the intricate relationship between music and consumers has become a critical endeavor. Whether it's the background music in a store, the jingles in advertisements, or the playlist in a restaurant, music plays a significant role in shaping consumer experiences and decision-making processes. In this section, we embark on a melodious journey into the psychology of music for the consumer, exploring how melodies, rhythms, and lyrics harmonize to influence moods, perceptions, and purchasing behaviors.

The emotional resonance of music is a central theme in the psychology of music for the consumer. Music has the remarkable ability to evoke a wide range of emotions, from joy and nostalgia to sadness and excitement. It taps into the limbic system of the brain, which is responsible for emotions, and triggers the release of neurotransmitters like dopamine and serotonin. As a result, music can directly impact consumers' emotional states.

Businesses harness this emotional power by carefully selecting music that aligns with their brand and the desired atmosphere of their spaces. For instance, a high-end boutique may opt for classical music to create an air of sophistication, while a lively cafe may play upbeat, energetic tunes to encourage a vibrant and welcoming environment. By choosing music that resonates with their target audience, businesses can enhance the overall consumer experience and influence perceptions.

Music has a profound connection with memory, and this bond

is integral to the psychology of music for the consumer. Certain songs or melodies can transport individuals back in time, evoking vivid memories and associated emotions. This phenomenon, known as the "music-evoked autobiographical memory effect," illustrates the power of music to trigger nostalgia and enhance the memorability of experiences.

In the context of marketing and branding, businesses strategically use music to create memorable associations with their products or services. Jingles in advertisements, for example, are designed to be catchy and easy to remember, ensuring that consumers recall the brand and its message. When music becomes intertwined with a brand's identity, it can reinforce consumer loyalty and recognition.

The role of music in regulating mood has significant implications for consumer behavior. Music can elevate mood, reduce stress, and even influence decision-making. Research has shown that consumers are more likely to spend time in stores with music that matches their emotional state or desired mood. For instance, soothing background music in a spa can enhance relaxation and encourage customers to stay longer and potentially spend more.

The tempo and rhythm of music can also influence the pace of consumer behavior. Fast-paced music may encourage quicker decision-making and impulse buying, while slower, more soothing music can promote a sense of leisure and encourage customers to explore products at a more relaxed pace. Retailers often use music strategically to create an optimal shopping environment that aligns with their business goals.

The choice of musical genre is a critical consideration in the psychology of music for the consumer. Different musical genres evoke distinct emotions and resonate with specific demographic groups. For example, classical music may appeal to an older, more sophisticated audience, while hip-hop or pop may connect with a younger, trendier demographic.

Businesses must carefully select musical genres that align with their target audience to create a meaningful connection. This choice extends to the branding and messaging of a business. For example, a sports retailer targeting a younger audience may use upbeat, energetic music in their marketing campaigns to reflect an active and dynamic lifestyle. The alignment of music and audience preferences enhances consumer engagement and brand affinity.

While music has the power to create positive and memorable experiences, businesses must also consider ethical considerations and sensitivity in their use of music. This includes obtaining appropriate licenses for music usage to respect copyright laws and supporting artists. Additionally, music should be chosen with cultural sensitivity in mind, especially in diverse markets, to avoid inadvertently alienating or offending consumers.

The volume of music in retail environments should be carefully controlled to ensure that it enhances the shopping experience rather than causing discomfort. Music should not interfere with communication between consumers and staff, and it should be at a level that allows customers to focus on their shopping experience without distraction.

The psychology of music for the consumer is a symphony of emotions, memories, and behaviors that harmonize to create meaningful and influential experiences. Music's ability to evoke emotions, trigger memories, regulate moods, and connect with specific target audiences makes it a powerful tool for businesses seeking to engage with consumers on a deeper level. However, the ethical use of music and sensitivity to individual preferences and cultural considerations are essential for creating a harmonious and enjoyable consumer experience. As businesses continue to explore the psychology of music, they will uncover new ways to use melodies, rhythms, and lyrics to foster brand loyalty, shape perceptions, and orchestrate delightful consumer interactions.

The Impact of Store Temperature
on Consumer Psychology

The temperature of a retail store is often an overlooked but crucial factor in shaping consumer psychology and behavior. Whether it's a scorching summer day or a chilly winter evening, the ambient temperature within a store can significantly influence how customers perceive the shopping experience and make purchasing decisions. In this section, we will explore into the multifaceted relationship between store temperature and consumer psychology, exploring the ways in which temperature affects mood, buying behavior, product evaluations, and overall satisfaction.

One of the most fundamental ways in which store temperature impacts consumer psychology is through its influence on mood. Psychologists have long established that environmental factors, including temperature, can evoke emotional responses. In a retail setting, a comfortable and pleasant temperature can uplift shoppers' moods, making them more receptive to engaging with products and the shopping environment. On the other hand, excessively hot or cold conditions can lead to discomfort, irritability, and even a desire to leave the store, affecting the overall shopping experience negatively. Retailers who understand this connection can strategically set store temperatures to create a positive shopping atmosphere that encourages longer visits and increased spending.

Store temperature also plays a vital role in influencing consumers' purchase decisions. Research has shown that warmer environments tend to increase impulsive buying behavior. Warmer temperatures can lead to a sense of relaxation and well-being, which can make shoppers more inclined to make unplanned purchases. Conversely, colder temperatures may encourage consumers to shop more cautiously, as they seek to minimize their time in the chilly environment. Understanding how temperature affects buying behavior can help retailers optimize their store environments to maximize sales.

The temperature of a store can impact how consumers perceive product quality. Warmer stores may lead consumers to perceive products as more attractive and appealing. For instance, clothing stores with slightly higher temperatures can make fabrics feel more comfortable, encouraging customers to try on garments and increasing the likelihood of purchase. On the contrary, cooler stores might lead customers to perceive products as durable and of higher quality, which can be advantageous for stores selling electronics, appliances, or luxury goods. Retailers must carefully consider the type of products they offer and how temperature can enhance or detract from their perceived quality.

The comfort level within a store directly correlates with how long customers are willing to stay and browse. Shoppers who feel comfortable in terms of temperature are more likely to explore the store, discover new products, and spend more time shopping. This extended dwell time provides retailers with more opportunities to engage with customers, offer assistance, and ultimately increase sales. A well-regulated store temperature can contribute to an inviting and enjoyable shopping experience that encourages customers to linger, boosting the chances of making a purchase.

Ultimately, the impact of store temperature on consumer psychology culminates in customer satisfaction and loyalty. Retailers who prioritize the comfort and preferences of their customers by maintaining an appropriate temperature can create a positive shopping experience that resonates with shoppers. Satisfied customers are more likely to return to the store and recommend it to others, fostering loyalty and contributing to long-term business success. Moreover, in an era of online shopping, providing a comfortable in-store experience can be a key differentiator that draws customers away from the convenience of e-commerce.

The temperature of a store is a powerful yet often underestimated factor in shaping consumer psychology and behavior. From influencing mood and purchase decisions to impacting product evaluations, dwell time, and overall customer satisfaction, temperature plays a pivotal role in the retail environment. Retailers who recognize the significance of this relationship and strategically manage store temperatures can enhance the shopping experience, increase sales, and build lasting customer loyalty. In an increasingly competitive retail landscape, understanding the psychological impact of store temperature is essential for thriving in the marketplace.

The Psychology of
Consumer Tangibility

I n the world of consumer psychology, the act of holding a product in one's hands stands as a pivotal moment in the purchase journey. This tangible connection between consumer and product is a potent force that influences decisions, preferences, and perceptions. It taps into the fundamental human need for sensory interaction, invoking emotions and impressions that can significantly shape the consumer's experience. In this exploration of the psychology behind this phenomenon, we transcend into the intricate web of emotions, senses, and perceptions that come into play when a consumer holds a product, unraveling the profound impact it has on the choices individuals make.

When a consumer reaches out to touch a product, an intricate sensory symphony unfolds. The tactile sense, in particular, plays a dominant role in this experience. The human hand is an incredibly sensitive organ, capable of discerning textures, temperatures, and shapes with remarkable precision. This tactile interaction goes beyond the mere physical contact; it elicits emotions and associations tied to these sensations. A smooth, cool surface might convey a sense of luxury, while a rough texture might evoke feelings of authenticity. These tactile cues trigger emotional responses that can either draw the consumer closer to the product or push them away.

Beyond tactile sensations, the act of holding a product fosters emotional connections. Psychologically, this tangible interaction activates a sense of ownership, even before the purchase has been made. Holding an item in one's hand allows the consumer to project themselves into a future scenario where they own and use the product. This projection stimulates positive emotions like satisfaction, joy, and anticipation. Marketers leverage this emotional resonance by crafting products with not just functionality but also aesthetics and design that elicit positive emotions. From the weight of a smartphone to the contours of a car's steering wheel, every aspect is meticulously designed to tap into the consumer's emotional psyche.

The psychology of holding a product extends its reach to the consumer's decision-making process. Studies have shown that when individuals physically handle a product, they are more likely to develop a sense of ownership and attachment. This attachment, in turn, makes it harder for them to part with the product without making a purchase. Furthermore, the act of touching a product can help consumers assess its quality, functionality, and suitability for their needs. It serves as a crucial information-gathering step, allowing consumers to bridge the gap between product features and their personal requirements. As such, this physical interaction often tips the scales in favor of making a purchase.

In the digital age, where online shopping has become the norm, the psychology of holding a product has undergone a transformation. E-commerce platforms have sought to replicate the tactile experience through augmented reality, 360-degree product views, and detailed product descriptions. However, these digital approximations still fall short of the tangible, multisensory experience of holding a physical product. Consumer psychology is continually evolving, and understanding how to evoke the same emotions and connections in a virtual setting remains a significant challenge. Nevertheless, the enduring power of holding a product in one's hands remains a testament to the profound impact of tactile interaction on consumer behavior, even in an increasingly digital world.

The Psychology of Store Layout

The layout of a retail store is far from arbitrary; it's a carefully designed strategic tool that influences consumer behavior and shapes the shopping experience. Store layout psychology explores into the art and science of how store environments are organized to engage and guide consumers. This section explores the psychology of store layout for the consumer, examining how elements such as store design, aisle arrangement, product placement, and sensory cues play a pivotal role in influencing consumer decisions, enhancing customer satisfaction, and ultimately driving sales.

The design of a store's physical space is the first point of contact between a consumer and a brand. It sets the stage for the entire shopping experience and can significantly impact a consumer's perception of the store and its products. Store design psychology emphasizes the importance of creating an inviting and aesthetically pleasing environment that resonates with the target audience.

Luxury retailers often use elegant, upscale designs with high-end materials and lighting to convey a sense of exclusivity and prestige. In contrast, discount stores may opt for simpler, cost-effective designs that emphasize value and affordability. The goal is to align the store's design with its brand image and target demographic to create a positive first impression.

Store layout also considers factors like traffic flow, accessibility, and sightlines. A well-designed store ensures that consumers can easily navigate the space, find products, and move smoothly from one area to another, enhancing the overall shopping experience.

Aisle arrangement is a fundamental aspect of store layout psychology. Retailers carefully plan how products are arranged on shelves and aisles to influence consumer behavior. A key strategy is to position high-demand or high-margin items at eye level, where they are most likely to catch a shopper's attention.

Endcaps, the shelves at the end of aisles, are prime real estate in stores. They are often used to showcase featured products, seasonal items, or promotions. The psychology here is to create a sense of urgency and encourage impulse purchases as shoppers pass by.

The arrangement of products on shelves can create cross-selling and upselling opportunities. Placing complementary products like peanut butter and jelly side by side encourages consumers to buy both, while offering a premium version of a product nearby can tempt consumers to trade up.

Product placement within a store layout has a profound impact on consumer decision-making. Retailers often strategically place products based on consumer psychology principles to optimize sales. One such principle is the "decoy effect," where a slightly less attractive option is positioned next to a more expensive one to make the latter appear as a better value.

Another tactic is to create product adjacency, placing related items near each other to simplify the shopping process and reduce decision fatigue. For example, placing pasta sauce and pasta in close proximity streamlines the shopping experience for consumers making a spaghetti dinner.

End-of-aisle displays, also known as "power aisles," often feature promotional items or best-sellers. These displays are designed to capture consumers' attention, encourage impulse purchases, and promote product discovery.

Store layout psychology goes beyond the visual and extends into the realm of sensory cues. Retailers recognize the power of sensory experiences in shaping consumer behavior and often leverage sound, scent, and tactile elements to create memorable shopping experiences.

Music, for instance, plays a crucial role in setting the tone of a store. Slow, soothing music can encourage consumers to linger and explore, while upbeat tunes can create a sense of excitement and urgency. Retailers may also use scent marketing, infusing the store with pleasant fragrances that evoke positive emotions and associations with the brand.

Tactile cues, such as product samples or interactive displays, engage consumers on a physical level and encourage hands-on exploration. These sensory experiences create a sense of connection with the products, increasing the likelihood of purchase.

Lighting is another powerful sensory tool. Well-planned lighting can enhance product visibility, highlight key areas, and create a welcoming atmosphere. Dimmed lighting in a fine dining section of a supermarket, for example, can evoke a sense of sophistication and relaxation.

The checkout area is the final frontier of store layout psychology. Retailers employ various strategies to encourage impulse purchases while consumers wait in line. These strategies include placing small, low-cost items like candies or magazines near the checkout, creating a last-minute temptation for shoppers.

Another checkout tactic is the use of loyalty programs, where consumers are prompted to join, earn rewards, or make additional purchases to save money or accrue points. This taps into the psychology of instant gratification and encourages shoppers to buy more to maximize their rewards.

Checkout lanes are often designed to guide consumers toward specific items. For example, a lane with a "10 items or less" sign may feature grab-and-go snacks and beverages, capitalizing on the convenience factor for consumers in a hurry.

Placing beer next to diapers in a retail store may seem like an unusual pairing, but it is rooted in the psychology of consumer behavior and shopping habits. This strategy is often employed to capitalize on the concept of convenience and the idea that shoppers frequently make unplanned or impulse purchases. By situating beer, a commonly purchased item, alongside diapers, a necessity for many parents, retailers aim to encourage dual purchases. Parents, who may have rushed into the store for diapers, are more likely to notice and consider purchasing beer when it is conveniently placed nearby. This seemingly random pairing leverages the psychology of shopping efficiency, making it more convenient for consumers and potentially boosting sales for both product categories.

Placing milk at the back of a grocery store is a strategic move grounded in the psychology of consumer behavior. This placement encourages shoppers to navigate through the entire store, exposing them to a wide range of products along the way. By making essential items like milk less accessible, retailers increase the likelihood that customers will encounter and purchase other products, potentially leading to impulse buys. Additionally, this design can enhance the overall shopping experience, as it allows customers to explore various sections of the store, discover new products, and potentially spend more time in the establishment. In essence, the psychology behind putting milk at the back of the store aligns with the retailer's goal of maximizing sales and customer engagement.

The psychology of store layout is a multifaceted field that combines elements of design, consumer behavior, and sensory cues to create an optimized shopping experience. By understanding the principles of store layout psychology, retailers can influence consumer decisions, enhance satisfaction, and ultimately drive sales. Store design, aisle arrangement, product placement, sensory cues, and checkout strategies all play integral roles in shaping the consumer's path to purchase. When executed effectively, these strategies create an environment where consumers feel comfortable, engaged, and motivated to make purchases, resulting in a successful and profitable retail experience.

The Psychology of Impulse Buying

Spontaneous purchases, often referred to as impulse buys, are a common occurrence in the world of consumer behavior. These unplanned and often sudden purchases can range from small items like snacks at the checkout counter to larger, more expensive products like electronics or clothing. Understanding the triggers and impulses behind spontaneous purchases is of great interest to businesses and marketers seeking to influence consumer behavior and boost sales. In this section, we will explore the psychological factors and triggers that drive spontaneous purchases, the role of emotional and situational influences, and strategies that businesses employ to capitalize on these impulses.

Spontaneous purchases are influenced by a variety of psychological triggers that tap into consumers' emotions, desires, and cognitive biases. Some of the key psychological triggers include:

Scarcity and Urgency: The fear of missing out (FOMO) is a potent trigger. Limited-time offers, flash sales, and phrases like "while supplies last" create a sense of urgency, compelling consumers to make quick decisions.

Social Proof: People tend to follow the behavior of others. When consumers see items marked as "bestsellers" or "trending," they may feel more inclined to make a purchase to align with the crowd.

Curiosity and Novelty: New or unique products, innovative features, or unusual packaging can pique consumers' curiosity and drive them to make impulsive purchases to satisfy that curiosity.

Emotional Appeal: Products that evoke strong emotions, such as happiness, nostalgia, or excitement, are more likely to trigger spontaneous purchases. Emotional advertising and storytelling play a significant role in this regard.

Discounts and Bargains: Perceived value is a powerful motivator. Discounts, promotions, and buy-one-get-one-free offers tap into consumers' desire to save money, prompting them to buy on the spot.

Instant Gratification: Many people seek immediate rewards. Products or services that offer instant gratification, such as fast food or downloadable content, cater to this impulse.

Understanding these psychological triggers allows businesses to strategically design marketing campaigns and in-store experiences that capitalize on consumers' natural inclinations.

Emotions play a significant role in spontaneous purchases. Consumers often make impulse buys based on how a product or experience makes them feel in the moment. Some emotional influences on impulse buying include:

Excitement: The thrill of discovering a new product or a great deal can trigger excitement, leading to impulsive purchases. Retailers often create an atmosphere of excitement through store displays and promotions.

Happiness: Positive emotions, such as happiness or joy, can drive impulsive purchases, especially for items that promise to enhance the consumer's mood or well-being.

Escape: Some consumers use impulse buying as a form of escape from stress or boredom. A spontaneous purchase can provide a momentary distraction or a sense of control over one's emotions.

Indulgence: Treating oneself to something special can be emotionally satisfying. Products associated with indulgence, such as luxury chocolates or spa treatments, often trigger impulse buys.

Desire for Change: The desire for change, novelty, or self-improvement can prompt spontaneous purchases of products or services that promise a new beginning or a better version of oneself.

Fear or Anxiety: On the flip side, fear of missing out or anxiety about scarcity can also be emotional triggers for impulse buying, as consumers rush to avoid perceived negative consequences.

Businesses can leverage emotional appeals in their marketing and advertising to create a strong connection between their products and the emotions consumers seek to experience.

Spontaneous purchases are often influenced by situational factors and contextual triggers that consumers encounter in their daily lives. Some of these factors include:

Store Layout and Merchandising: Retailers strategically place products near checkout counters, end-caps, and other high-traffic areas to catch the eye of shoppers and encourage impulse buys.

Proximity and Accessibility: Products that are conveniently located and easy to access are more likely to be spontaneously purchased. This is why items like gum, candy, and magazines are often near the cash register.

Time Constraints: When consumers are in a hurry or pressed for time, they may be more susceptible to making impulsive decisions rather than carefully weighing their options.

In-Store Promotions: In-store promotions, such as product demonstrations, samples, or limited-time discounts, can trigger unplanned purchases as consumers take advantage of immediate opportunities.

Social Context: Shopping with friends or family members can influence spontaneous purchases. Peer pressure or the desire to keep up with others may lead to impulsive buying decisions.

Online Shopping: In the digital realm, one-click purchasing and personalized recommendations on e-commerce websites can facilitate impulse buys.

Understanding the situational factors that contribute to impulse buying allows businesses to design retail spaces and online shopping experiences that maximize their influence on consumer behavior.

Businesses employ a range of strategies to encourage and capitalize on spontaneous purchases. Some of these strategies include:

Point-of-Purchase Displays: Eye-catching displays near checkout counters or in-store entrances feature products likely to trigger impulse purchases. These displays often highlight discounts or limited-time offers.

Cross-Selling and Upselling: Recommending related or complementary products during the checkout process can prompt customers to add additional items to their purchase.

Limited-Time Offers: Time-limited promotions and flash sales create a sense of urgency, motivating consumers to act quickly.

Remarketing and Retargeting: Online retailers use cookies and data analysis to deliver personalized ads and product recommendations to shoppers, reminding them of products they viewed previously.

Abandoned Cart Strategies: Businesses send reminders and incentives to customers who have abandoned their online shopping carts, encouraging them to complete their purchases.

Loyalty Programs: Offering rewards or discounts to loyal customers can motivate them to make additional purchases.

Influencer Marketing: Collaborating with influencers who have a large and engaged following can introduce products to new audiences and trigger impulse buys.

Employing these strategies effectively requires a deep

understanding of consumer behavior and the ability to create compelling marketing campaigns and shopping experiences.

It's important to recognize that impulse buying is often an emotional and spontaneous process. However, after making an impulse purchase, consumers may engage in post-purchase rationalization, where they seek to justify their decision.

Confirmation Bias: Consumers may actively seek out information that confirms the wisdom of their impulse purchase while ignoring or downplaying contradictory information.

Attribution of Value: Consumers may find additional value or utility in the purchased item that was not initially apparent, reinforcing their belief in the decision.

Emotional Attachment: The positive emotions associated with the impulse purchase may lead to a sense of attachment to the product, further justifying the decision.

Sunk Cost Fallacy: Consumers may perceive the money spent on the impulse purchase as a sunk cost and feel compelled to use or enjoy the product to avoid feeling wasteful.

Understanding this post-purchase rationalization process is important for businesses because it can influence consumers' future buying decisions and brand loyalty. Positive post-purchase experiences and satisfaction can lead to repeat business and even word-of-mouth recommendations, while negative experiences can have the opposite effect.

Situational factors, including store layout, time constraints, and social contexts, play a crucial role in influencing spontaneous purchases. Businesses can optimize these factors to create environments conducive to impulsive buying.

To capitalize on spontaneous purchases, businesses employ a range of strategies, from point-of-purchase displays to loyalty programs and influencer marketing. These tactics are designed to leverage the triggers and impulses that drive consumers to make unplanned purchases.

It is essential to recognize that consumer decision-making is not solely impulsive; it also involves post-purchase rationalization. This process can further solidify consumer loyalty or lead to dissatisfaction, making it vital for businesses to provide positive post-purchase experiences and support.

Understanding the triggers and impulses behind spontaneous purchases is a complex and multifaceted endeavor. Successful businesses are those that grasp the psychological, emotional, and situational factors at play and employ effective strategies to engage consumers and drive impulse buying behavior.

The Psychology of Pricing and Discounts

Pricing is a critical component of any business strategy, and understanding the psychology behind pricing and discounts is essential for influencing consumer behavior and driving sales. Consumers don't make purchasing decisions based solely on objective factors like production costs; they are also influenced by psychological cues and perceptions related to pricing. In this section, we will explore the intricate world of the psychology of pricing and discounts, delving into the various pricing strategies, the impact of perception, and the role of discounts in shaping consumer choices.

Pricing strategies are designed to influence how consumers perceive the value of a product or service. Several key strategies are commonly used to achieve this effect:

Psychological Pricing: This strategy involves setting prices just below round numbers (e.g., $9.99 instead of $10.00) to create the perception of a better deal. Consumers tend to focus on the leftmost digits, associating the price with the lower value.

Prestige Pricing: Higher prices are often associated with higher quality or exclusivity. Businesses use prestige pricing to position their products or services as premium offerings. For example, luxury brands consistently use higher price points to convey prestige.

Price Anchoring: By presenting a higher-priced option alongside a target product, businesses create an anchor point that influences consumers' perception of value. The target product appears more reasonable in comparison.

Odd-Even Pricing: Odd pricing (e.g., $19.99) suggests value and affordability, while even pricing (e.g., $20.00) conveys quality and simplicity. Businesses choose between these approaches based on their brand positioning and target market.

Bundle Pricing: Offering products or services as a bundle can make the overall price seem more attractive than purchasing individual items separately. This strategy leverages the principle of perceived value.

These pricing strategies leverage consumers' psychological biases and perceptions to influence their decisions and encourage purchases.

The decoy effect is a powerful psychological principle used in pricing strategies. It involves introducing a third, less attractive option (the decoy) to make a target option seem more appealing. This concept is closely related to choice architecture, which explores how the presentation of options influences decisions.

For example, imagine a menu at a restaurant:

Option A: Small Soda for $1

Option B: Medium Soda for $2

Option C: Large Soda for $2.50

Here, Option B is the decoy. It makes Option C (the target option) appear more attractive because it's only $0.50 more expensive but significantly larger. Customers are more likely to choose Option C over Option A, thanks to the presence of the decoy.

The decoy effect and choice architecture are widely used in pricing and marketing to guide consumers toward specific choices, maximizing sales and profitability.

Discounts play a significant role in consumer decision-making. The psychology behind discounts revolves around the appeal of saving money. Several principles influence the perception of discounts:

Loss Aversion: Humans are naturally averse to losses. Discounts trigger the fear of missing out on a good deal, motivating consumers to make purchases to avoid losing the opportunity.

Anchoring: As mentioned earlier, anchoring involves presenting a higher-priced original price alongside a discounted price. Consumers anchor their perception of value to the original price, making the discount appear more substantial.

Percentage vs. Absolute Discounts: Consumers often prefer percentage discounts over absolute discounts because they perceive a higher percentage as a better deal, even if the actual savings may be smaller.

Limited-Time Offers: The concept of scarcity and urgency is closely tied to discounts. Limited-time offers create a sense of urgency, driving consumers to take immediate action to secure the discounted price.

Bulk Discounts: Discounts for buying in bulk tap into consumers' desire to save money per unit. The more they buy, the greater the perceived savings.

Businesses use these principles to structure their discount strategies effectively, enticing consumers to make purchases and boosting sales.

Consumers often perceive higher-priced products as higher in quality. This perception is known as price-value perception. Businesses use this psychological bias to their advantage by pricing products strategically to convey quality and value.

A restaurant may offer two bottles of wine: one priced at $20 and another at $50. Most consumers will assume that the $50 bottle is of higher quality, even if they have limited knowledge of wine. This perception influences their purchasing decision, and many will choose the more expensive option.

It's crucial for businesses to maintain a balance between price and actual quality. If customers perceive a significant disconnect between the two, it can erode trust and lead to dissatisfaction.

Bundling, upselling, and cross-selling are pricing and sales strategies that leverage the psychology of value and choice. These strategies involve offering complementary products or services alongside the main product to encourage consumers to spend more or make additional purchases.

Bundling: Bundling combines related products or services at a single price point, often at a lower cost than purchasing them separately. This strategy creates the perception of value and encourages consumers to buy the bundle.

Upselling: Upselling involves offering a higher-priced version of a product or service with additional features or benefits. Consumers are enticed to spend more to gain enhanced value or convenience.

Cross-Selling: Cross-selling recommends related or complementary products or services at the point of purchase. This strategy capitalizes on consumers' existing purchase decisions and their willingness to explore additional offerings.

These strategies work by appealing to consumers' desire for convenience, added value, or enhanced experiences. They leverage the psychology of incremental spending, where customers are more likely to justify spending a bit more when they perceive the added value as worthwhile.

The psychology behind dealerships using random numbers for pricing is a strategic attempt to create an impression of fairness, transparency, and unpredictability in the minds of consumers. When pricing seems arbitrary or unrelated to traditional numerical patterns, it can give the illusion that the dealership is offering a unique and unbiased deal. Additionally, the use of random numbers can make it challenging for consumers to compare prices easily, as there may be no clear reference point. This can lead buyers to rely more on perceived value, subjective assessments, and their trust in the dealership. However, consumers should be cautious, as the appearance of randomness does not always equate to fair pricing, and it's essential to conduct thorough research and negotiation before making a purchasing decision.

The psychology of pricing and discounts is a complex and fascinating field that directly impacts consumer behavior and purchasing decisions. Businesses that understand the various pricing strategies, the influence of perception, and the power of discounts are better equipped to tailor their pricing strategies to maximize sales and profitability.

Effective pricing strategies involve tapping into consumers' natural biases and perceptions, using psychological cues to create the perception of value, quality, and savings. The presence of discounts, presented strategically, can trigger the fear of missing out and motivate consumers to make purchases.

The principles of choice architecture, anchored pricing, and the decoy effect are powerful tools in guiding consumers toward specific choices, whether in a restaurant menu or an e-commerce platform. Bundling, upselling, and cross-selling leverage the psychology of incremental spending, allowing businesses to increase the average transaction value and enhance overall profitability.

In conclusion, businesses that master the psychology of pricing and discounts can not only boost sales and revenue but also build stronger customer relationships by aligning their pricing strategies with consumer perceptions and preferences. As consumer behavior continues to evolve, a deep understanding of pricing psychology remains a key driver of success in the modern marketplace.

Perception and Attention

Consumer perception and information processing are critical aspects of the decision-making process in today's dynamic marketplace. As consumers are constantly bombarded with a vast amount of information, understanding how they perceive and process this information is essential for businesses and marketers. In this section, we will dive into the intricacies of how consumers perceive and process information, exploring the cognitive and psychological factors that influence their decision-making. By gaining insights into these processes, businesses can better tailor their marketing strategies and products to meet the ever-evolving needs and preferences of consumers.

Perception is the initial stage of information processing and plays a fundamental role in shaping consumer decisions. It refers to how individuals interpret and make sense of the sensory information they receive from their environment. The human brain is bombarded with an overwhelming amount of stimuli every second, and perception helps filter and prioritize this information.

One of the key concepts in perception is selective attention, where consumers focus on certain stimuli while ignoring others. This selectivity is influenced by factors such as personal interests, needs, and previous experiences. Marketers often try to capture consumers' attention through advertising, packaging, and branding to ensure their products or messages are noticed in the noisy marketplace. Understanding what captures a consumer's attention can help businesses design more effective marketing campaigns.

Perception is also influenced by perceptual biases, which can lead consumers to perceive products or information in ways that align with their existing beliefs and attitudes. For example, confirmation bias can cause consumers to seek out information that confirms their preconceived notions, while cognitive dissonance theory explains how consumers may reinterpret information to reduce discomfort when their choices don't align with their values. Recognizing these biases can assist marketers in crafting persuasive messages that resonate with their target audience.

Once consumers have perceived information, the next step is information processing. Information processing involves mentally organizing, encoding, and storing information for future use. The process is influenced by cognitive factors such as memory, learning, and decision-making heuristics.

Memory plays a crucial role in information processing, as consumers need to remember and recall information to make informed decisions. Short-term memory is limited in capacity and duration, so marketers must present information in a way that facilitates its transfer to long-term memory. Strategies like repetition, storytelling, and using vivid imagery can enhance memory retention.

Consumers often rely on decision-making heuristics, which are mental shortcuts or rules of thumb, to simplify complex choices. For instance, the availability heuristic leads consumers to make decisions based on the information that is readily available to them. Marketers can leverage this by ensuring their products or messages are easily accessible and memorable.

Emotions play a significant role in how consumers perceive and process information. Emotional responses can influence decision-making, sometimes even more than rational considerations. Consumers are more likely to make purchases when they have positive emotional experiences with a brand or product. Therefore, understanding and evoking the right emotions through marketing campaigns and product experiences can be a powerful tool for businesses.

Psychological factors such as motivation, attitude, and personality also shape information processing. Motivation determines the degree of effort consumers are willing to invest in processing information. High motivation may lead to more thorough information processing, while low motivation can result in superficial processing or even information avoidance. Marketers can increase motivation through incentives, rewards, and compelling storytelling.

Attitudes, which are a combination of beliefs, feelings, and behavioral intentions, influence how consumers process information related to a product or brand. Businesses often engage in attitude change strategies to shift consumer perceptions in their favor. This may involve leveraging cognitive dissonance theory or appealing to emotional and social motives.

Personality traits can also impact information processing. For example, individuals with high openness to experience may be more receptive to novel products and information, while those with a high need for cognitive closure may prefer straightforward, well-organized information. Tailoring marketing messages to align with different personality traits can enhance their effectiveness.

The digital age has ushered in significant changes in how consumers perceive and process information. The internet and smartphones have made information more accessible than ever before, leading to shorter attention spans and increased multitasking. As a result, marketers must adapt their strategies to capture and retain consumer attention in a digital landscape.

Social media platforms, in particular, have become powerful tools for information dissemination and brand engagement. They offer opportunities for user-generated content, influencer marketing, and real-time interactions with consumers. Understanding how different demographic groups use and engage with social media can help businesses tailor their strategies for maximum impact.

The rise of e-commerce has changed the way consumers gather information about products and make purchase decisions. Online reviews and ratings, for instance, play a significant role in shaping consumer perceptions. Negative reviews can deter potential buyers, while positive reviews can boost trust and confidence. Businesses need to actively manage their online reputation and engage with customers to ensure a positive online presence.

Consumer perception and information processing are complex and multifaceted processes that significantly influence purchasing decisions. To succeed in today's competitive marketplace, businesses and marketers must be attuned to the cognitive, emotional, and psychological factors that shape these processes.

Tailoring marketing strategies to capture consumers' attention, leveraging emotional appeals, and understanding the role of technology in information dissemination are all essential considerations. Additionally, recognizing the impact of individual differences, such as personality traits and attitudes, can help marketers craft messages and experiences that resonate with diverse audiences.

By gaining a deeper understanding of how consumers perceive and process information, businesses can create more effective marketing campaigns, develop products that meet consumer needs, and ultimately foster stronger customer relationships in an ever-evolving consumer landscape.

In addition to the aforementioned strategies, it's vital for marketers to adopt a customer-centric approach. This means continuously listening to and understanding consumer feedback, preferences, and evolving needs. Tools like surveys, focus groups, and data analytics can provide invaluable insights into consumer behavior and perception, enabling businesses to adapt and refine their strategies in real-time.

Personalization is another key element in modern marketing. Leveraging data-driven personalization techniques allows businesses to deliver tailored content and product recommendations to individual consumers. This not only enhances the overall shopping experience but also increases the likelihood of conversion.

Ethical considerations in marketing are becoming increasingly important. Consumers are more conscious of issues like data privacy, transparency, and sustainability. Marketers need to communicate their commitment to these values and align their practices accordingly to build trust and loyalty among consumers.

Understanding how consumers perceive and process information is a fundamental aspect of successful marketing in today's dynamic and competitive landscape. By recognizing the role of perception, the impact of emotions and psychology, the influence of technology, and the need for personalization and ethical practices, businesses can develop more effective strategies that resonate with consumers and drive long-term success.

It's important to remember that consumer behavior and information processing are not static; they evolve over time, influenced by societal changes, technological advancements, and shifting cultural norms. Therefore, staying agile and adaptable in response to these changes is crucial for marketers aiming to remain relevant and connect with consumers in meaningful ways.

In an era where consumer choices are abundant, and the flow of information is constant, those businesses that excel in understanding and harnessing the intricacies of consumer perception and information processing will be better equipped to thrive and build lasting relationships with their customers.

In the ever-evolving landscape of marketing, businesses constantly seek innovative ways to capture the attention of their target audience and leave a lasting impression. Understanding the intricacies of human perception, sensory cues, and attention is paramount in this endeavor. This section explores into the pivotal role that sensory cues and attention play in modern marketing. It explores how businesses leverage sensory stimuli to create memorable brand experiences, examines the psychological mechanisms behind attention, discusses the challenges of capturing and maintaining consumer focus in an increasingly cluttered world, and provides insights into the future of sensory marketing in the digital age.

Sensory cues are the gateway to a consumer's perception of a brand or product. These cues encompass various sensory modalities, including visual, auditory, olfactory, tactile, and gustatory stimuli. In marketing, the visual sense often takes center stage, as it allows for the creation of compelling logos, advertisements, and packaging designs. A well-designed visual identity can communicate a brand's values, evoke emotions, and foster recognition. For example, the iconic red and white of Coca-Cola, the golden arches of McDonald's, and the swoosh of Nike are all visual cues that instantly evoke specific emotions and associations in consumers' minds.

Other senses play crucial roles as well. Auditory cues, such as jingles and brand-specific sounds, can reinforce brand recognition and elicit positive emotions. Think of Intel's "Intel Inside" jingle, which has become synonymous with high-performance computing. Similarly, olfactory cues, like the scent of freshly baked bread in a bakery, can trigger cravings and enhance the overall shopping experience. The strategic use of sensory cues allows businesses to create a multi-sensory brand experience that resonates deeply with consumers.

Attention is a limited cognitive resource, and understanding its psychology is pivotal in marketing. The human brain is bombarded with an overwhelming amount of information daily, making selective attention crucial. Attention is typically divided into two main types: bottom-up and top-down.

Bottom-up attention is involuntary and stimulus-driven. It occurs when a sensory cue captures our attention without conscious effort. For example, a sudden loud noise or a bright, eye-catching color can divert our attention, making us focus on the source of the stimulus. In marketing, this can be seen in attention-grabbing advertisements or displays that use bold colors and striking visuals to stand out in a crowded marketplace.

On the other hand, top-down attention is more controlled and goal-oriented. It involves consciously directing one's attention to specific information or stimuli based on personal goals, interests, or intentions. In marketing, this type of attention can be harnessed through targeted advertising campaigns that cater to consumers' interests and needs. For instance, an online clothing retailer might use data analysis to recommend products based on a customer's browsing history, effectively capturing their top-down attention.

In an era of information overload, capturing and maintaining consumer attention has become increasingly challenging. The average attention span of humans has been steadily decreasing, making it crucial for marketers to adapt their strategies. One of the primary challenges is overcoming banner blindness and ad fatigue, where consumers automatically filter out and ignore digital advertisements due to their ubiquity.

Another challenge lies in the ever-growing competition for attention across various media channels. Social media, streaming platforms, and mobile apps constantly vie for user engagement, making it imperative for marketers to create content that not only grabs attention but also holds it. This has given rise to the importance of storytelling and creating narratives that resonate with consumers on a personal level.

The ethical dimension of attention manipulation has gained prominence. Marketers must strike a balance between capturing attention ethically and respecting consumers' autonomy. Practices such as clickbait and dark patterns can lead to short-term gains but damage a brand's long-term reputation.

As technology continues to advance, the role of sensory cues and attention in marketing is poised for further transformation. Virtual reality (VR) and augmented reality (AR) technologies offer new opportunities to engage consumers on a multi-sensory level, immersing them in brand experiences that feel real and memorable. For instance, a furniture retailer can use AR to allow customers to visualize how a piece of furniture would look in their own home before making a purchase.

The integration of artificial intelligence and machine learning enables more personalized and context-aware marketing efforts. Chatbots and virtual assistants can interact with consumers in real-time, providing customized recommendations and information, effectively capturing top-down attention.

In conclusion, sensory cues and attention are central to the world of marketing. Businesses that understand the power of sensory stimuli and the psychology of attention can create compelling brand experiences that resonate with consumers. However, the challenges of capturing and maintaining attention in a cluttered digital landscape require constant adaptation and ethical considerations. As technology continues to evolve, the future of sensory marketing promises even more immersive and personalized experiences, ushering in a new era of consumer engagement.

Memory and Learning

Memory and learning are integral aspects of human cognition that play a profound role in shaping consumer behavior and choices. Understanding how individuals remember information, acquire knowledge, and apply it when making purchasing decisions is fundamental for businesses seeking to succeed in today's competitive markets. In this section, we will explore the intricate relationship between memory, learning, and consumer choices. We will look into the cognitive processes that underlie memory and learning, examine how these processes influence consumers at various stages of the decision-making process, and discuss the implications for marketing strategies and product development. Memory and learning are interconnected cognitive processes that involve the acquisition, storage, and retrieval of information. Learning is the process through which individuals acquire new knowledge or skills, while memory refers to the retention and recall of that knowledge over time. These processes are highly interdependent, as learning is often facilitated by memory, and memory is enhanced through learning.

The human memory system consists of multiple components, including sensory memory, short-term memory, and long-term memory. Sensory memory briefly holds sensory information such as sights, sounds, and smells. Short-term memory retains information for a brief period, while long-term memory stores information for an extended duration, potentially for a lifetime. Learning typically involves encoding new information in short-term memory and transferring it to long-term memory through processes like rehearsal, elaboration, and consolidation.

Memory and learning impact consumer choices at various stages of the decision-making process. In the initial stage of problem recognition, consumers draw upon their memory to identify needs or desires based on past experiences or learned preferences. For example, if a person remembers enjoying a particular brand of coffee in the past, this memory may trigger a desire for that brand when they recognize a need for coffee.

Familiarity and recognition play significant roles in consumer choices. Brands that consumers have encountered repeatedly or have learned about through advertising and marketing efforts tend to enjoy an advantage. This is because familiarity enhances the ease of processing information, making it more likely for consumers to choose a recognized brand over an unfamiliar one, even if they cannot recall specific details about the product.

Learning and memory also influence how well consumers retain product information. Information that is encoded effectively in memory, often through repetition or emotional connections, is more likely to be remembered and considered during the decision-making process. Effective marketing strategies often employ techniques that enhance the encoding of product information in consumers' long-term memory.

Consumers frequently employ mental shortcuts or heuristics to simplify complex decisions. These heuristics often rely on memory and learning. For example, the availability heuristic involves basing judgments on readily available information from memory. If consumers easily remember positive experiences with a product, they may use this information to infer its overall quality.

Memory and learning continue to influence consumer choices after the purchase. Consumers store memories of their experiences with a product and use this information to inform future decisions. Positive experiences may lead to brand loyalty and repeat purchases, while negative experiences can deter consumers and influence them to explore alternatives.

Understanding the role of memory and learning in consumer choices has significant implications for marketing strategies and product development:

Branding and Recognition: Businesses can invest in branding efforts to enhance recognition and familiarity, making their products more accessible in consumers' memory. Consistent branding across various touchpoints can reinforce recognition.

Product Information Presentation: Marketers should present product information in ways that facilitate encoding in long-term memory. This may involve using storytelling, emotional appeals, or repetition to make the information more memorable.

Feedback and Post-Purchase Engagement: Companies should prioritize post-purchase engagement to create positive memories and encourage repeat business. Soliciting feedback and addressing customer concerns can improve the overall consumer experience.

Educational Marketing: Providing consumers with valuable information and knowledge about products or services can aid in the learning process. Educational marketing materials can help consumers make more informed choices.

Personalization: Leveraging data-driven personalization allows businesses to tailor their marketing messages and product recommendations to individual consumers, aligning with their specific preferences and past behaviors.

Memory and learning are foundational cognitive processes that shape consumer choices at every stage of the decision-making process. Understanding how individuals acquire, store, and retrieve information is crucial for businesses seeking to create effective marketing strategies and products that resonate with their target audience. By appreciating the complex interplay between memory, learning, and consumer choices, companies can design more compelling campaigns, build stronger brand loyalty, and ultimately thrive in the competitive marketplace.

In today's saturated marketplace, creating memorable brand experiences has become imperative for businesses seeking to stand out and forge deep connections with consumers. Beyond delivering a product or service, memorable brand experiences engage emotions, foster loyalty, and leave a lasting imprint in the minds of customers. In this section, we explore strategies that empower brands to craft remarkable experiences that resonate with their target audience. We traverse into the importance of storytelling, the role of personalization, the value of consistency, the impact of sensory engagement, and the significance of community-building in creating memorable brand experiences.

At the heart of creating memorable brand experiences lies the art of storytelling. Stories have the unique ability to captivate, connect, and convey a brand's values and identity in a relatable and engaging manner. To harness the power of storytelling:

Define Your Brand Narrative: Begin by defining your brand's narrative, which should encapsulate your mission, values, and vision. This narrative becomes the backbone of your storytelling efforts.

Embrace Authenticity: Authenticity is the key to resonating with audiences. Share genuine stories that reflect your brand's history, challenges, and successes. Transparency builds trust.

Create Emotional Connections: Stories that evoke emotions are more likely to be remembered. Appeal to feelings like joy, nostalgia, or empathy to make your brand experience unforgettable.

Consistency in Messaging: Maintain a consistent narrative across all touchpoints, from social media to product packaging, to reinforce the brand's story and make it a part of the consumer's memory.

Personalization is a potent tool in creating memorable brand experiences. Today's consumers expect brands to understand their individual needs and preferences. To achieve personalization:

Data-Driven Insights: Leverage data analytics to gain insights into consumer behavior and preferences. This information enables you to tailor marketing efforts and product recommendations.

Dynamic Content: Create dynamic content that adapts to individual consumers. Personalized emails, product recommendations, and customized offers can significantly enhance the customer experience.

Emotional Intelligence: Understand the emotional context of customer interactions. Empathetic responses and personalized communication can leave a profound impact.

Interactive Engagement: Develop interactive experiences, such as quizzes or surveys, that allow customers to engage with your brand on a personal level. These interactions are more likely to be memorable.

Consistency is a cornerstone of memorable brand experiences. When consumers encounter consistent messaging, design, and values across various touchpoints, it reinforces the brand's identity and creates a cohesive experience. To ensure consistency:

Establish Brand Guidelines: Create comprehensive brand guidelines that outline visual identity, messaging tone, and core values. Share these guidelines with your team and partners.

Monitor All Channels: Regularly audit all brand touchpoints, including social media, websites, print materials, and customer service interactions, to ensure they align with the established guidelines.

Train Your Team: Educate your employees and partners about the importance of consistency and provide them with the tools and knowledge to uphold brand standards.

Evolve with Purpose: While consistency is vital, brands should also evolve strategically. Ensure that any changes align with the brand's core narrative and values.

Engaging multiple senses can create rich and memorable brand experiences. Sensory cues, such as visuals, sounds, scents, and textures, can evoke powerful emotions and associations. To leverage sensory engagement:

Visual Identity: Invest in visually appealing design that conveys your brand's personality. Colors, typography, and imagery should align with your narrative.

Audio Branding: Develop a unique audio identity, such as a distinctive jingle or sound logo, to reinforce brand recognition through auditory cues.

Scent and Taste: Consider incorporating scent and taste experiences, particularly in physical retail environments. Scent marketing and tastings can create strong sensory associations.

Haptic Feedback: Pay attention to tactile experiences, especially in product design. The feel and texture of products can influence perceptions of quality and value.

Creating a sense of community around your brand can be a powerful way to foster memorable experiences. Building a community around shared values, interests, or aspirations can lead to increased loyalty and advocacy. To build a brand community:

Define Your Brand Community: Identify the shared interests, values, or passions that resonate with your target audience and align with your brand. This forms the basis for your community.

Social Media Engagement: Use social media platforms to facilitate conversations, share user-generated content, and connect with your community.

Exclusive Events and Content: Offer exclusive events, content, or perks to community members to reward their loyalty and make them feel special.

Storytelling within the Community: Encourage community members to share their own stories and experiences related to your brand. User-generated content can be a powerful form of storytelling.

Crafting memorable brand experiences requires a strategic blend of storytelling, personalization, consistency, sensory engagement, and community building. These strategies allow brands to create meaningful connections with their audience, leaving indelible imprints in the minds and hearts of consumers. By prioritizing these elements and continually evolving to meet changing consumer expectations, businesses can build lasting relationships and thrive in a competitive marketplace, where memorable experiences often define success.

Motivation and Emotion

C onsumer behavior is a complex interplay of various psychological, social, and economic factors. At its core, however, lies the powerful driving force of motivation. Understanding the motivations behind consumer choices is crucial for businesses seeking to tailor their marketing strategies, product offerings, and customer experiences to meet the needs and desires of their target audience. In this section, we delve into the fundamental motivational factors that drive consumer behavior, exploring how internal and external motives influence purchasing decisions and the implications for businesses in today's dynamic marketplace.

Intrinsic motivation refers to the internal desires and needs that drive individuals to engage in activities or make choices for their own sake, rather than for external rewards or incentives. In the realm of consumer behavior, intrinsic motivation plays a significant role in guiding purchasing decisions. Several key intrinsic motives include:

Self-Expression: Consumers often seek products that allow them to express their identity, values, or personality. For example, someone who values sustainability may be intrinsically motivated to buy eco-friendly products as a means of self-expression.

Self-Improvement: The desire for personal growth and improvement can motivate consumers to invest in products or services that contribute to their well-being. This includes purchases related to fitness, education, or self-help.

Enjoyment and Pleasure: Many consumer choices are driven by the intrinsic motivation to experience joy and pleasure. This can involve indulgent purchases such as fine dining, luxury vacations, or entertainment.

Autonomy and Control: Some consumers are motivated by the desire for autonomy and control over their lives. Products that offer customization or personalization cater to this intrinsic motivation.

Understanding intrinsic motivation enables businesses to create products and marketing messages that resonate with consumers on a deeper level. Brands that align with consumers' intrinsic values and aspirations can build strong emotional connections and foster loyalty.

While intrinsic motivations are driven by internal desires, extrinsic motivation stems from external rewards or incentives. Extrinsic motivators can significantly impact consumer behavior, and businesses often employ various strategies to leverage these motives. Key forms of extrinsic motivation in consumer behavior include:

Discounts and Promotions: Offering discounts, promotions, or special offers can stimulate purchases by providing consumers with tangible cost savings or value-added benefits.

Loyalty Programs: Loyalty programs and rewards schemes incentivize repeat purchases by offering tangible rewards, such as points, discounts, or exclusive access to products or services.

Social Recognition: External validation and recognition from peers and society can be a powerful motivator. Products that are associated with social status or prestige often tap into this extrinsic motivation.

Competition: Consumer behavior can be influenced by competitive motives, such as the desire to outdo others or achieve a sense of accomplishment. Limited-edition releases or exclusive products can fuel this competitive drive.

Extrinsic motivators are frequently used by businesses to drive short-term sales and engagement. However, it is essential for companies to strike a balance between extrinsic and intrinsic motivations, as overreliance on external rewards can undermine long-term customer loyalty and satisfaction.

Emotions play a significant role in consumer behavior, driving choices that are often based on feelings and affective states. Businesses that understand the emotional motivations behind consumer behavior can create compelling marketing campaigns and customer experiences. Key emotional motives include:

Happiness and Joy: Consumers are often motivated to make purchases that bring them happiness and joy. Products that evoke positive emotions, such as gifts, entertainment, or comfort food, align with this motivation.

Fear and Anxiety: On the other hand, consumers may be motivated to address fears and anxieties. Products or services that offer security, safety, or peace of mind cater to this emotional motivation.

Nostalgia: Nostalgia-driven motivation taps into consumers' longing for the past. Products that evoke feelings of nostalgia, such as retro designs or classic flavors, can be highly appealing.

Empathy and Altruism: Some consumers are motivated by a sense of empathy and altruism. They seek out products or brands that support social causes, sustainability, or ethical practices.

Businesses can harness emotional motivation by creating emotional connections with their audience through storytelling, empathetic marketing, and aligning their brand values with the emotional needs and desires of consumers.

Human beings are inherently social creatures, and social motivation often plays a pivotal role in consumer behavior. This motivation is driven by the desire for social belonging, conformity, and the need to be part of a larger community. Key social motives include:

Social Influence: Consumers are influenced by the behavior and opinions of others, whether friends, family, or online communities. Social proof, such as positive reviews and testimonials, can sway consumer choices.

Conformity: The desire to conform to societal norms and expectations can shape consumer behavior. Brands that align with prevailing cultural trends and values can appeal to this motivation.

Social Identity: Consumers often seek products or experiences that reinforce their social identity or group affiliation. For example, sports fans may buy team merchandise to express their allegiance.

Belongingness: The need for social belonging and connection drives consumers to engage with brands and products that foster a sense of community and inclusion.

Understanding social motivation allows businesses to create marketing strategies that tap into the desire for social connection and belonging. Building online communities, encouraging user-generated content, and fostering brand advocacy are effective ways to leverage social motivation.

While emotions and social influences are powerful drivers of consumer behavior, rational motivation also plays a significant role. Rational motives are rooted in logic, utility, and the assessment of benefits and costs. Key rational motives include:

Cost-Benefit Analysis: Consumers often engage in a cost-benefit analysis when making purchases. They weigh the perceived benefits of a product or service against its price and perceived value.

Product Features and Functionality: Consumers assess the features, functionality, and utility of a product to determine if it meets their practical needs and expectations.

Information and Education: Rational consumers seek

information and education about products or services before making decisions. Providing clear and accurate product information is essential.

Problem Solving: Consumers may be motivated to address specific problems or challenges in their lives. Products or services that offer effective solutions cater to this rational motivation.

Businesses can leverage rational motivation by providing transparent information, highlighting product features and benefits, and offering solutions that align with consumers' practical needs.

Consumer behavior is driven by a multitude of motivational forces, each influencing choices in distinct ways. These motivations encompass intrinsic and extrinsic desires, emotional and social needs, as well as rational considerations. Businesses that understand the intricate interplay of these motivational factors can tailor their marketing strategies, product offerings, and customer experiences to meet the diverse needs and desires of their target audience. By connecting with consumers on a deeper level and addressing their specific motivations, brands can foster customer loyalty, drive sales, and create lasting relationships in today's dynamic marketplace.

The world of consumer behavior is a complex and fascinating arena where rationality and emotions frequently collide. While logic and practicality certainly play roles in purchasing decisions, it is emotions that often exert a profound and decisive influence. Emotions can shape the way consumers perceive, evaluate, and ultimately choose products or services. In this section, we will explore the multifaceted impact of emotions on purchasing decisions, examining how various emotional states influence consumer behavior, the mechanisms behind emotional decision-making, the role of branding and marketing in eliciting emotions, the potential pitfalls of emotional decision-making, and strategies businesses can employ to harness the power of emotions effectively.

Emotions encompass a wide spectrum of feelings, from joy and excitement to fear and anger. Each emotion can influence purchasing decisions differently, often depending on the context and individual preferences. Here are some key emotions and their impact on consumer behavior:

Joy and Excitement: Positive emotions like joy and excitement can lead to impulsive purchases, often driven by the desire to experience pleasure or happiness. Marketers leverage these emotions to create a sense of urgency and delight, particularly during sales or promotions.

Fear and Anxiety: Negative emotions, such as fear and anxiety, can drive consumers to seek solutions or products that offer security or alleviate discomfort. Products like insurance, home security systems, or health-related items tap into these emotions.

Trust and Confidence: Feelings of trust and confidence can lead to brand loyalty. Consumers are more likely to choose products from brands they trust, and these emotional connections often result from consistent positive experiences.

Nostalgia and Sentimentality: Emotions tied to nostalgia and sentimentality can drive purchases related to cherished memories or a desire to relive the past. Brands that evoke nostalgia, such as classic or retro products, can be highly appealing.

Guilt and Altruism: Guilt can drive consumers to make ethical or responsible choices, such as buying eco-friendly or socially responsible products. Altruistic emotions play a role in supporting charitable causes or contributing to social good.

Understanding the emotional spectrum allows businesses to tailor their marketing strategies, product positioning, and customer experiences to evoke specific emotions that align with their offerings.

Emotional decision-making involves a combination of cognitive and affective processes. Several key mechanisms underlie the impact of emotions on purchasing decisions:

Affect Heuristic: The affect heuristic is a mental shortcut in which individuals rely on their emotional responses to evaluate and make decisions about products or situations. When a product elicits positive emotions, consumers are more likely to perceive it as favorable and make a purchase.

Emotional Contagion: Emotions can be contagious, spreading from one person to another. Positive emotions generated by engaging advertisements or positive customer interactions can influence purchasing decisions through emotional contagion.

Emotional Memory: Emotions are often linked to memory formation. Consumers are more likely to remember and recall products associated with strong emotional experiences. This can lead to brand loyalty and repeat purchases.

Emotional Decision Threshold: Emotions can act as decision thresholds, tipping the balance when consumers are on the fence about a purchase. When emotions align with the desire to buy, consumers are more likely to proceed.

Emotional Priming: Marketers use emotional priming techniques to influence consumer behavior by exposing them to emotionally charged stimuli before presenting a product or offer. This primes consumers' emotional states and can affect their decision-making.

Understanding these mechanisms enables businesses to design marketing campaigns and customer experiences that effectively tap into consumers' emotional responses and drive desired purchasing decisions.

Branding and marketing strategies play a central role in eliciting emotions that influence purchasing decisions. Businesses invest significant efforts in crafting emotional connections with their target audience. Key tactics include:

Storytelling: Brands often use storytelling to create narratives that resonate with consumers' emotions. Compelling stories can evoke empathy, excitement, or nostalgia and build emotional bonds with the brand.

Visual and Sensory Elements: Visual design, colors, imagery, and sensory cues can evoke emotions. For example, vibrant colors may create excitement, while calming visuals can induce a sense of tranquility.

Emotional Appeals: Emotional appeals in advertising, such as humor, fear, or empathy, are designed to provoke emotional responses that drive action. These appeals can be highly effective in shaping purchasing decisions.

User-Generated Content: Encouraging customers to share their own emotional experiences with a product or brand can create a sense of community and authenticity, fostering emotional connections.

Personalization: Personalized marketing that caters to individual preferences and behaviors can elicit emotions related to feeling valued and understood.

Effective branding and marketing strategies align the emotional messaging with the product or service's core value proposition, creating a seamless and emotionally resonant customer experience.

While emotions can be powerful drivers of purchasing decisions, they are not without their pitfalls. Emotional decision-making can lead to impulsive choices, buyer's remorse, or susceptibility to manipulative marketing tactics. Some common pitfalls include:

Impulsivity: Overwhelming emotions can lead to impulsive decisions that consumers may later regret. Impulsive purchases driven by momentary excitement or fear may not align with long-term goals.

Manipulative Marketing: Some marketing tactics exploit consumers' emotions for short-term gains, leading to deceptive or unethical practices that erode trust and brand reputation.

Emotional Bias: Emotions can bias perception and judgment, leading consumers to overlook important product attributes or make decisions based solely on emotional appeal rather than practical utility.

Emotional Manipulation: Excessive use of emotional appeals without providing transparent information can lead to manipulation and dissatisfaction when consumers feel they were misled.

To avoid these pitfalls, businesses should strike a balance between emotional appeals and rational information, ensuring that consumers have access to clear, accurate, and complete product information.

Businesses can harness the power of emotions effectively by employing various strategies:

Emotional Intelligence: Develop emotional intelligence within the organization to understand customer emotions and empathize with their needs and concerns.

Customer Journey Mapping: Map the customer journey to identify touchpoints where emotional connections can be strengthened, such as during onboarding, customer support interactions, or post-purchase follow-ups.

Storytelling Mastery: Invest in storytelling techniques that create authentic narratives connecting with consumers' emotions, values, and aspirations.

Ethical Marketing: Prioritize ethical marketing practices that respect consumers' emotions and provide truthful and transparent information.

Emotional Feedback Loop: Create mechanisms for customers to provide emotional feedback, enabling businesses to continuously improve their emotional connections.

The impact of emotions on purchasing decisions is a dynamic and multifaceted phenomenon. Emotions influence consumers at various stages of their decision-making journey, from initial awareness to post-purchase satisfaction. Businesses that understand the emotional motives behind consumer behavior and employ strategies to evoke the right emotions can build strong emotional connections, foster brand loyalty, and drive successful long-term relationships with their customers. In today's competitive marketplace, where consumers often have countless choices, the ability to resonate with emotions is a key differentiator that can lead to enduring success and customer loyalty.

Environmental and Sustainable Consumer Behavior

I n recent years, environmental and sustainable consumer behavior has gained significant attention and importance as individuals and societies become more aware of the urgent need to address environmental challenges such as climate change, resource depletion, and pollution. The way consumers make choices about what they buy, use, and dispose of has a profound impact on the environment. This section explores into the complex and multifaceted realm of environmental and sustainable consumer behavior, exploring its underlying factors, motivations, challenges, and the potential for transformative change. By examining the interplay of individual choices and broader societal influences, we aim to shed light on the path towards a greener and more sustainable future.

Environmental and sustainable consumer behavior can be defined as the choices individuals make regarding the purchase, use, and disposal of products and services with consideration for their environmental and social impact. It encompasses a wide range of decisions, from selecting energy-efficient appliances to buying locally sourced food or supporting eco-friendly brands. These choices reflect an individual's values, beliefs, and attitudes toward environmental sustainability. Understanding this behavior requires an exploration of its underlying factors.

Personal Values and Beliefs: One of the primary drivers of sustainable consumer behavior is an individual's personal values and beliefs. People who prioritize environmental and social issues are more likely to make sustainable choices. This alignment of values with behavior is often referred to as "green consumerism."

Knowledge and Awareness: Environmental literacy and awareness play a crucial role in shaping consumer behavior. Informed consumers are more likely to make environmentally conscious choices. Access to information through media, education, and marketing campaigns can significantly impact consumer knowledge.

Economic Considerations: Sustainable choices are sometimes driven by economic factors. Energy-efficient appliances, for instance, can lead to cost savings in the long run. However, the initial investment required for sustainable products can be a barrier for some consumers.

Environmental Concerns: Concern for the environment, including issues like climate change, deforestation, and plastic pollution, is a powerful motivator for sustainable behavior. People often choose eco-friendly products to reduce their ecological footprint.

Social Responsibility: Consumers increasingly view their purchasing decisions as a means to contribute to socially responsible causes. Supporting businesses that prioritize fair labor practices, ethical sourcing, and community development can be a motivating factor.

Peer Influence and Social Norms: Social pressure and the desire to conform to societal norms can shape consumer behavior. If sustainable choices become the norm within a community or social group, individuals are more likely to follow suit.

While many individuals express interest in environmental and sustainable consumer behavior, there are several challenges and barriers that hinder widespread adoption of such practices.

Price and Accessibility: Sustainable products often come with a higher price tag due to their production methods and materials. This price barrier can deter lower-income consumers from making environmentally friendly choices.

Limited Choice: In some regions or markets, consumers may have limited access to sustainable products and services, making it difficult to make environmentally conscious choices.

Greenwashing: Some businesses engage in "greenwashing," which involves making false or exaggerated claims about the environmental benefits of their products. This can mislead consumers and erode trust in sustainability claims.

Psychological Distance: The concept of "psychological distance" suggests that people tend to prioritize immediate concerns over distant, long-term issues like environmental sustainability. This cognitive bias can hinder sustainable decision-making.

Consumer Behavior Inertia: People often stick to familiar routines and habits, even if they are aware of more sustainable alternatives. Breaking these patterns can be challenging.

Businesses play a pivotal role in shaping consumer behavior and fostering sustainability. By adopting environmentally friendly practices and offering sustainable products, they can influence consumer choices in several ways.

Product Innovation: Companies can develop and market products that are both sustainable and appealing to consumers. Innovations such as electric vehicles, renewable energy technologies, and eco-friendly packaging have the potential to drive sustainable consumer behavior.

Transparency and Accountability: Transparency in supply chains and sustainability reporting can build trust with consumers. Businesses that demonstrate a commitment to ethical and sustainable practices are more likely to attract environmentally conscious consumers.

Consumer Behavior in Healthcare and Wellness

Consumer choices in the realm of health and well-being are influenced by a complex interplay of psychological, emotional, and cognitive factors. Decisions regarding healthcare, diet, exercise, and lifestyle are not solely driven by objective medical information; they are deeply rooted in individual beliefs, emotions, and perceptions. Understanding the psychology behind health-related consumer choices is crucial for healthcare providers, policymakers, and wellness industries to better support individuals in making informed and healthy decisions. In this section, we will explore the intricate psychology of health-related consumer choices, including the role of risk perception, the influence of emotions, the impact of social factors, and strategies for promoting positive health behaviors.

Risk perception is a fundamental psychological factor that shapes health-related consumer choices. How individuals perceive risks associated with various health behaviors or conditions profoundly influences their decisions. Several key aspects of risk perception include:

Perceived Susceptibility: Individuals assess their personal vulnerability to health risks. Those who believe they are at higher risk for a particular condition may be more motivated to take preventive actions, such as regular health check-ups or adopting healthier lifestyles.

Perceived Severity: The perceived severity of a health condition impacts decision-making. Consumers are more likely to take action if they perceive the consequences of an illness as severe or life-altering.

Perceived Benefits vs. Perceived Barriers: Consumers weigh the perceived benefits of a health behavior or intervention against the perceived barriers. If the perceived benefits outweigh the barriers, individuals are more inclined to engage in the behavior.

Temporal Discounting: People often discount future risks in favor of immediate gratification. This can lead to unhealthy choices, such as indulging in unhealthy foods or avoiding exercise.

Framing Effects: The way health information is framed can significantly impact risk perception. Positive framing emphasizes the benefits of a health behavior, while negative framing highlights the risks of not taking action.

Understanding how individuals perceive and interpret health-related risks is essential for developing effective interventions and communication strategies.

Emotions play a substantial role in health-related consumer choices. Emotions can either motivate or hinder healthy behaviors, depending on the specific emotional response. Some key emotional factors include:

Fear and Anxiety: Fear of illness or health complications can drive individuals to seek healthcare services, adopt preventive measures, or change unhealthy habits. Anxiety about one's health status can serve as a powerful motivator for health behavior change.

Hope and Optimism: Positive emotions like hope and optimism can encourage individuals to pursue healthier lifestyles. Hope for improved well-being or a better quality of life can be a strong incentive.

Stress and Coping Mechanisms: Stress can lead to both healthy and unhealthy coping mechanisms. Some may turn to stress eating or smoking, while others may engage in stress-reducing activities like exercise or mindfulness.

Guilt and Shame: Negative emotions like guilt and shame can result from unhealthy behaviors. These emotions can serve as motivators for change or, conversely, lead to further unhealthy behaviors as a means of coping with emotional distress.

Satisfaction and Self-Efficacy: Positive emotions resulting from achieving health-related goals, such as weight loss or quitting smoking, can reinforce healthy behaviors and boost self-efficacy.

Recognizing the emotional aspects of health decisions allows healthcare professionals and wellness industries to provide emotional support, motivation, and tailored interventions to address emotional barriers to health behavior change.

Social influences and interpersonal relationships have a significant impact on health-related consumer choices. People are influenced by the behaviors, attitudes, and norms of those around them. Key social factors include:

Social Norms: Individuals often conform to perceived social norms related to health behaviors. For example, if it is perceived as normal within a social group to engage in regular exercise or maintain a healthy diet, individuals are more likely to adopt these behaviors.

Social Support: Positive social support from friends, family, or support groups can encourage and facilitate health behavior change. Conversely, negative social support or discouragement can hinder progress.

Peer Pressure: Peer pressure can influence health choices, both positively and negatively. Pressure from peers to engage in unhealthy behaviors can be a barrier, while encouragement to adopt healthier habits can be a motivator.

Role Models: Having positive role models who exemplify healthy behaviors can inspire individuals to make similar choices.

Social Comparison: People often compare themselves to others regarding health and fitness. This can lead to motivation for improvement or negative self-perception and discouragement.

Recognizing the impact of social factors allows for the development of interventions and campaigns that leverage social influences to promote positive health behaviors.

Cognitive biases are systematic patterns of deviation from norm or rationality in judgment, often leading to perceptual distortion or illogical interpretation. Several cognitive biases can impact health-related consumer choices:

Confirmation Bias: Individuals tend to seek out information that confirms their pre-existing beliefs or choices. This can lead to selective exposure to information that supports unhealthy behaviors.

Availability Heuristic: People tend to rely on readily available information when making decisions. If information about a particular health behavior or treatment is easily accessible, it may disproportionately influence decision-making.

Optimism Bias: Individuals often underestimate their own risk of experiencing negative health outcomes, believing that such outcomes are more likely to happen to others.

Anchoring: The initial information encountered can act as an anchor that influences subsequent decisions. For example, the presentation of a specific treatment option as the first choice can anchor a patient's perception of treatment effectiveness.

Status Quo Bias: Many people prefer to maintain their current habits and are resistant to change, even when presented with information about healthier alternatives.

Recognizing these cognitive biases is essential for healthcare providers and wellness industries to counteract them through patient education, decision aids, and behavioral nudges.

Promoting positive health behaviors requires a nuanced approach that considers the psychology of consumer choices.

Effective strategies include:

Behavioral Nudges: Employing behavioral economics principles, such as default options or incentives, to encourage healthier choices.

Health Education: Providing clear, accurate, and accessible information to empower individuals to make informed decisions about their health.

Social Support: Creating supportive communities and networks to encourage and reinforce healthy behaviors.

Emotional Support: Recognizing the emotional challenges associated with behavior change and offering emotional support and coping strategies.

Normative Feedback: Providing individuals with feedback on their health behaviors compared to social norms or peer groups to motivate positive change.

Cognitive Bias Mitigation: Developing interventions that address cognitive biases, such as presenting information in a balanced way to counter confirmation bias.

Personalized Interventions: Tailoring interventions to individual preferences, goals, and psychological profiles to enhance engagement and effectiveness.

In conclusion, understanding the psychology of health-related consumer choices is essential for promoting positive health behaviors and facilitating informed decisions. By recognizing the role of risk perception, emotions, social factors, cognitive biases, and employing effective strategies, healthcare providers and wellness industries can empower individuals to make healthier choices and improve overall well-being.

Cognitive Biases in Consumer Decision-Making

C onsumer choices are not always driven by purely rational and objective factors. Instead, they are often influenced by cognitive biases—systematic errors in judgment and decision-making that arise from the brain's inherent shortcuts and heuristics. These biases, deeply rooted in human psychology, can significantly impact the way individuals perceive products, brands, and purchasing decisions. In this section, we will explore five common cognitive biases that influence consumer choices, understand their underlying mechanisms, and discuss how businesses can leverage this understanding to create more effective marketing strategies and improve customer engagement.

Confirmation bias is the tendency to seek, interpret, and remember information in a way that confirms one's existing beliefs or preconceptions while avoiding information that contradicts them. In consumer behavior, this bias can lead individuals to selectively gather and remember information that aligns with their prior opinions or preferences. For instance, a person already favoring a particular brand may actively seek out positive reviews or ignore negative ones, reinforcing their belief in the brand's superiority.

Businesses can leverage confirmation bias by aligning their marketing efforts with consumers' existing beliefs or preferences. This involves understanding the target audience's values and opinions and crafting messaging that reinforces those beliefs. However, it's important to strike a balance between leveraging confirmation bias and maintaining ethical and truthful marketing practices. Overly biased or deceptive tactics can damage trust and brand reputation.

Anchoring bias occurs when individuals rely too heavily on the first piece of information encountered (the "anchor") when making decisions. This initial information often serves as a reference point, influencing subsequent judgments. In consumer choices, anchoring can lead people to make decisions based on the first price they see, whether it's high or low. For example, when consumers encounter a high-priced luxury item first, they may perceive subsequent, lower-priced items as more affordable, even if the prices are still relatively high.

Businesses can use anchoring to their advantage by strategically presenting initial information to influence consumer perceptions. For instance, when offering multiple pricing options, placing a higher-priced option first can make the lower-priced options appear more attractive. However, this should be done transparently and ethically, as deceptive anchoring tactics can erode trust.

Scarcity bias, also known as the scarcity principle, occurs when people place a higher value on items or opportunities that are perceived as scarce or limited in availability. When consumers believe that a product is in short supply or available for a limited time, they often experience a heightened sense of urgency and are more motivated to make a purchase. For example, online retailers frequently use phrases like "limited stock" or "only a few left" to create a sense of scarcity and encourage immediate buying.

To harness scarcity bias, businesses can implement strategies such as limited-time promotions, exclusive releases, or creating the perception of scarcity through marketing tactics. However, it is essential to maintain transparency and authenticity when employing scarcity tactics to avoid undermining consumer trust.

Social proof is the tendency to rely on the behavior and opinions of others as a guide for our own actions and decisions.

In consumer behavior, social proof plays a significant role, influencing choices through factors like peer recommendations, product reviews, and social media endorsements. When individuals see others positively interacting with a product or brand, they are more likely to follow suit. For instance, a restaurant with a long line outside often attracts more customers because people assume it must be worth the wait due to the social proof of others waiting.

Businesses can harness social proof by encouraging customer reviews, testimonials, and user-generated content. Displaying the positive experiences of previous customers can build trust and influence potential buyers. Additionally, highlighting the popularity or widespread adoption of a product can enhance its perceived value.

The endowment effect is the cognitive bias that leads individuals to assign a higher value to objects or items they already own compared to those they do not possess. In consumer choices, this bias can manifest when individuals hesitate to sell an item at its market value because they perceive it as more valuable to them personally. It can also lead to reluctance to switch brands or products due to an emotional attachment to the current choice.

Businesses can navigate the endowment effect by creating a sense of ownership or attachment among their customers. Loyalty programs, personalized recommendations, and exclusive offers can strengthen customers' attachment to a brand or product. However, businesses should be cautious not to exploit this bias through manipulative tactics that harm consumer interests.

Cognitive biases are prevalent and pervasive in consumer choices, influencing how individuals perceive, evaluate, and decide on products, brands, and purchasing decisions. Businesses that understand these biases and their underlying mechanisms can develop more effective marketing strategies, optimize customer engagement, and enhance the overall consumer experience. While leveraging cognitive biases can be beneficial, it is essential to do so ethically, transparently, and in a way that builds trust and long-term customer relationships. Recognizing the role of biases in consumer behavior is a valuable tool for businesses seeking to succeed in today's dynamic marketplace.

Consumer decision-making is often influenced by cognitive biases, systematic errors in judgment and decision-making rooted in human psychology. Marketers have long recognized the power of these biases in shaping consumer choices and have developed strategies to both leverage and counteract them. In this section, we will explore how marketers can strategically leverage cognitive biases to enhance their marketing efforts, increase conversion rates, and foster customer loyalty. Additionally, we will discuss ethical considerations and the importance of transparency when utilizing cognitive biases in marketing strategies.

Confirmation bias, which involves seeking and interpreting information that confirms existing beliefs, can be leveraged by marketers to reinforce consumers' positive perceptions of their products or brands. Strategies to consider include:

User-generated content: Encourage satisfied customers to share their experiences through reviews, testimonials, or social media posts. These positive endorsements align with consumers' pre-existing beliefs in the brand's value.

Selective highlighting: Emphasize aspects of your product or service that align with your target audience's beliefs or preferences. This helps confirm existing positive perceptions and reinforces the decision to choose your brand.

Content alignment: Craft marketing content that resonates with consumers' values and opinions. When your messaging aligns with their beliefs, it encourages confirmation bias and strengthens their connection with your brand.

Anchoring bias, the tendency to rely heavily on the first piece of information encountered, can be a powerful tool in pricing and product positioning. Marketers can strategically use anchoring to influence consumer decisions:

Price anchoring: Display a higher-priced product or option first to anchor consumers' expectations. Subsequently presenting lower-priced alternatives can make them appear more affordable and attractive.

Tiered pricing: Offer multiple pricing tiers with the highest-priced tier first. Consumers are more likely to choose a middle-tier option when it appears as a compromise between the anchor and the lowest-tier option.

Discount anchoring: Show the original price alongside the discounted price to anchor the perceived value of the discount. This can make consumers feel like they are getting a better deal.

While leveraging cognitive biases can be effective, marketers also have a responsibility to counteract biases that may lead to unethical or manipulative practices. Here are strategies to counteract cognitive biases in marketing:

Counter confirmation bias and anchoring bias by providing transparent, balanced, and accurate information to consumers. This includes:

Disclosure of limitations: Clearly communicate any limitations, potential downsides, or negative aspects of your product or service in marketing materials and on your website.

Full product information: Provide comprehensive product information, including specifications, features, and pricing details, so consumers can make informed decisions without relying solely on biases.

Objective reviews: Encourage and display both positive and negative reviews, offering a balanced view of the consumer experiences with your product or service.

Emphasize ethical marketing practices that prioritize consumer welfare over short-term gains:

Avoid deceptive tactics: Steer clear of manipulative tactics that exploit cognitive biases at the expense of consumer well-being, trust, or financial interests.

Honesty and authenticity: Build your brand on honesty, transparency, and authenticity. This helps counteract biases associated with skepticism and mistrust.

Consumer education: Educate consumers about common cognitive biases and how to recognize them. Providing awareness empowers consumers to make more rational decisions.

Encourage consumers to take control of their decision-making process by offering choice and autonomy:

Clear product comparisons: Provide tools and resources for consumers to compare products or services based on their own criteria, reducing reliance on anchoring bias.

Customization options: Offer customization features that allow consumers to personalize their choices, reducing the impact of biases related to conformity or one-size-fits-all solutions.

Opt-out alternatives: Ensure that consumers can easily opt out of marketing emails, subscriptions, or promotions. Respect their choices and preferences.

Marketers can ethically leverage cognitive biases to enhance their strategies by adhering to principles that prioritize consumer well-being and transparency:

Focus on creating genuine value for consumers through products, services, and marketing efforts. When consumers perceive value in what you offer, cognitive biases can enhance their satisfaction and loyalty.

Facilitate informed decision-making by providing comprehensive and accurate information. Help consumers understand the implications of their choices, reducing the potential impact of biases like confirmation and anchoring.

Use cognitive biases ethically to persuade rather than manipulate. Ensure that your marketing efforts align with consumers' best interests and respect their autonomy.

Be transparent about your marketing tactics, pricing strategies, and the information you present to consumers. Transparency fosters trust and mitigates biases associated with suspicion or skepticism.

Collect and act upon consumer feedback to continually improve your marketing strategies and products. Feedback helps identify areas where cognitive biases may be influencing decision-making and allows for adjustments to align with consumer preferences.

Consumer education is a valuable tool for both leveraging and counteracting cognitive biases. Marketers can play a role in educating consumers about common biases, helping them make more informed choices. Strategies for consumer education include:

Content and resources: Provide educational content on your website or in marketing materials that explains cognitive biases, their impact on decision-making, and how consumers can recognize and address them.

Workshops and webinars: Host workshops or webinars on consumer psychology and decision-making biases. Invite experts to share insights and practical tips.

Collaborative efforts: Collaborate with consumer advocacy organizations or educational institutions to promote consumer education on biases and ethical marketing practices.

By promoting consumer education, businesses can foster transparency, build trust, and empower consumers to make more rational, informed decisions while also increasing awareness of their own marketing tactics.

Cognitive biases are powerful forces in consumer decision-making, shaping perceptions, preferences, and choices. Marketers have the opportunity to leverage these biases ethically to enhance their strategies, but they must also be diligent in countering biases that may lead to unethical or manipulative practices. By prioritizing transparency, ethical marketing, consumer education, and the creation of genuine value, marketers can create a win-win situation where consumers benefit from more informed choices, and businesses thrive through increased customer loyalty and trust.

Social Influence and
Group Dynamics

Consumer behavior is a multifaceted field influenced by a wide array of factors, and social factors play a central and enduring role in shaping how individuals make choices in the marketplace. These social factors encompass various aspects of human interactions, including culture, social class, reference groups, family, and social influence. In this section, we will dive into the complex interplay of social factors in consumer behavior, exploring how they impact product preferences, purchasing decisions, and overall consumer experiences. Understanding these dynamics is crucial for businesses seeking to connect with their target audiences and tailor their marketing strategies effectively.

Culture is a pervasive and deeply ingrained social factor that significantly impacts consumer behavior. Cultural factors encompass shared values, beliefs, customs, norms, and traditions within a society or group. Culture shapes consumers' preferences, perceptions, and behaviors in various ways:

Product Preferences: Cultural values and beliefs influence what products or services are considered desirable or appropriate. For instance, in cultures that prioritize health and wellness, organic and natural products may have higher demand.

Communication Styles: Culture dictates communication norms and etiquette. Effective marketing strategies must align with cultural communication styles to resonate with consumers.

Symbolism and Meaning: Products can carry symbolic meanings within a culture. For example, the color red may symbolize good luck in some cultures and love in others, affecting product design and marketing messages.

Purchase Rituals: Cultural rituals and traditions often dictate when and how consumers make purchases, such as gift-giving during holidays or specific ceremonies.

To succeed in culturally diverse markets, businesses must conduct thorough cultural research, adapt their marketing messages, and respect cultural sensitivities.

Social class, often defined by income, education, occupation, and lifestyle, has a profound influence on consumer behavior. Individuals from different social classes have varying purchasing habits and preferences:

Luxury vs. Necessity: Social class can determine whether a product is perceived as a luxury or a necessity. High-income consumers may view luxury goods as status symbols, while lower-income consumers prioritize essential items.

Brand Preferences: Social class can influence brand preferences. Consumers from higher social classes may favor premium or designer brands, while those from lower social classes may prioritize value or generic options.

Shopping Habits: Social class can dictate where and how consumers shop. High-income individuals may frequent upscale boutiques, while lower-income individuals may shop at discount stores.

Aspirational Purchases: Social class can lead to aspirational purchases, where consumers from lower social classes buy products associated with higher social strata to elevate their status.

Understanding the social class of their target audience allows businesses to tailor marketing strategies, pricing, and product offerings to align with consumers' social and economic backgrounds.

Reference groups are social groups or communities to which

individuals belong or aspire to belong. These groups exert a significant influence on consumer behavior through various mechanisms:

Normative Influence: Reference groups set social norms and standards that guide consumer behavior. Individuals often conform to the preferences and choices of their reference groups to gain acceptance and approval.

Informational Influence: Reference groups provide information and recommendations about products or services. Word-of-mouth recommendations from reference groups can be highly persuasive.

Aspirational Influence: Consumers may aspire to belong to or emulate the lifestyles of their reference groups. This aspiration can lead to purchasing decisions that align with the group's values and preferences.

Dissociative Influence: In contrast, consumers may distance themselves from reference groups whose values or behaviors they disagree with. This can lead to avoidance of certain products or brands.

Identifying and understanding the reference groups that influence a target audience enables businesses to create marketing strategies that resonate with consumers' desire for belonging, acceptance, and alignment with their chosen communities.

Family is a fundamental social factor that significantly shapes consumer behavior. Family dynamics, roles, and relationships impact various aspects of consumer choices:

Decision-Making Roles: Within a family, different members may play distinct roles in decision-making. Marketers must consider who the primary decision-maker is for specific products or services.

Influence of Children: Children often influence family

purchasing decisions, particularly for products like toys, electronics, and food. Understanding children's preferences and desires is essential for marketing to families.

Interpersonal Communication: Family members communicate and share information about products and brands. Positive word-of-mouth within families can lead to increased brand loyalty and adoption.

Cultural and Generational Factors: Family traditions, cultural backgrounds, and generational influences shape preferences and expectations, impacting product choices and brand loyalty.

Businesses targeting families should recognize the complexities of family dynamics and tailor marketing efforts to resonate with the needs and preferences of different family members.

Social influence, the process by which people's attitudes, beliefs, and behaviors are affected by the presence or actions of others, plays a central role in consumer behavior. Social influence mechanisms include:

Peer Pressure: Consumers may make purchasing decisions to conform to the behaviors and preferences of their peers or social networks.

Social Proof: Demonstrating that others have had positive experiences with a product or service through testimonials, reviews, or endorsements can build trust and encourage adoption.

Authority Influence: Consumers often trust and follow the recommendations of authoritative figures, experts, or celebrities.

Scarcity and FOMO (Fear of Missing Out): The perception of limited availability or popularity of a product can create a sense of urgency and drive consumers to make purchases to avoid missing out on a perceived opportunity.

Online Social Networks: Social media platforms have become

powerful tools for social influence. Consumers often turn to social media for product recommendations, reviews, and endorsements from peers and influencers.

Marketers can leverage social influence by incorporating elements such as user-generated content, influencer collaborations, and social proof in their marketing strategies. Harnessing the power of social networks and peer interactions can lead to increased brand awareness, engagement, and conversions.

Social factors are integral to understanding and influencing consumer behavior. Culture, social class, reference groups, family dynamics, and social influence all play significant roles in shaping consumers' preferences, perceptions, and purchasing decisions. Businesses that recognize the complexities of these social factors and adapt their marketing strategies accordingly are better positioned to connect with their target audiences, build trust, and foster brand loyalty.

It is essential to approach the influence of social factors ethically and responsibly. Marketing should respect diverse cultural backgrounds, uphold ethical standards, and prioritize consumer well-being. Moreover, businesses should continuously adapt to evolving social dynamics and consumer preferences to remain relevant and successful in today's dynamic marketplace. By appreciating the multifaceted nature of social factors, businesses can forge meaningful connections with consumers and thrive in an increasingly interconnected world.

Word-of-mouth marketing, social proof, and groupthink have emerged as influential drivers of consumer behavior and decision-making. These phenomena tap into the fundamental human desire for social validation, guidance, and conformity. We will traverse into the dynamics of word-of-mouth marketing, social proof, and groupthink, exploring their impact on consumer choices, the strategies businesses employ to leverage these forces, the potential risks of manipulation and misinformation, and the ethical considerations surrounding these practices.

Word-of-mouth marketing (WOMM) refers to the practice of individuals sharing their opinions, experiences, and recommendations about products or services with others in their social circles. It relies on the inherent trust and credibility associated with personal recommendations, making it a potent tool for businesses seeking to build brand awareness and foster consumer trust.

The Power of Authenticity: Authenticity is a cornerstone of WOMM. Consumers tend to trust recommendations from friends, family, or peers because they believe these individuals have no ulterior motives. This trust can lead to a higher likelihood of trying a recommended product or service.

Digital Amplification: The advent of social media and online review platforms has transformed WOMM into a digital phenomenon with the potential for global reach. Positive reviews, ratings, and user-generated content can amplify the impact of word-of-mouth recommendations.

Leveraging Influencers: Businesses often collaborate with influencers—individuals with large and engaged social media followings—to disseminate their products or services through authentic, influencer-driven recommendations.

Effective WOMM strategies involve encouraging satisfied customers to share their experiences, creating shareable content, and monitoring online conversations to respond to feedback and address concerns promptly.

Social proof is a psychological phenomenon wherein individuals look to others, especially peers or a larger group, to guide their own decisions and actions. It operates on the premise that if many others are doing something, it must be the correct or advisable course of action. Marketers leverage social proof to build trust and credibility around their offerings.

Types of Social Proof: Various forms of social proof exist, including user reviews and ratings, celebrity endorsements, expert endorsements, social media likes and shares, and the display of product popularity (e.g., "bestseller" labels).

The Bandwagon Effect: Social proof often leads to the bandwagon effect, where people follow the prevailing trend or popular choice, even if it does not align with their individual preferences or needs.

Reducing Uncertainty: Social proof helps consumers reduce uncertainty and make decisions more efficiently, especially when faced with numerous options or unfamiliar choices.

To harness social proof effectively, businesses must cultivate positive online reviews, collaborate with reputable experts or celebrities, and create persuasive marketing materials that highlight the popularity and approval of their products or services.

While word-of-mouth marketing and social proof can be powerful tools for businesses, they are not without potential pitfalls. Groupthink, a related concept, highlights the risks associated with excessive conformity and uncritical adoption of prevailing views within a group. Groupthink occurs when a group values harmony and consensus over critical thinking and alternative viewpoints. It often results in decisions or actions that are misguided or irrational.

Consumer Implications: In the context of consumer behavior, groupthink can lead individuals to make purchasing decisions based solely on the prevailing opinions within their social circles, ignoring their own preferences and critical evaluation.

Herd Behavior: Groupthink can contribute to herd behavior, where individuals blindly follow the choices of others without independent analysis. This behavior can lead to market bubbles, overhyped products, or fads.

Businesses should be cautious about inadvertently promoting

groupthink by respecting consumer autonomy, avoiding manipulative tactics, and encouraging open dialogue and critical thinking among their audience.

As businesses increasingly seek to harness word-of-mouth marketing and social proof, there are concerns about the potential for manipulation and misinformation. When used unethically, these tactics can erode trust and harm consumers. Some risks include:

Fake Reviews: The proliferation of fake reviews on online platforms can deceive consumers and lead them to make ill-informed decisions. Businesses should combat fake reviews by reporting them and ensuring that their own marketing practices are transparent and honest.

Influencer Disclosure: Collaboration with influencers should be transparent, with clear disclosure of paid partnerships. Failure to do so can mislead consumers and damage trust.

Confirmation Bias: Consumers may seek out and believe only the information that confirms their existing beliefs or preferences. This can lead to echo chambers where misinformation is perpetuated.

To mitigate these risks, businesses should prioritize transparency, authenticity, and ethical practices in their marketing efforts. They should also support measures to combat misinformation and promote media literacy among consumers.

Ethical considerations are paramount in the use of word-of-mouth marketing, social proof, and related strategies. Businesses have a responsibility to engage in responsible marketing practices that respect consumer autonomy and well-being. Ethical principles include:

Transparency: Businesses should be transparent about their marketing practices, partnerships, and the presentation of user-generated content. This transparency helps consumers make informed decisions.

Respect for Autonomy: Consumers have the right to make choices based on their individual preferences, needs, and values. Businesses should avoid manipulative tactics that undermine this autonomy.

Accuracy and Honesty: Marketers should provide accurate and honest information about their products or services, avoiding deceptive claims or practices.

Consumer Welfare: The well-being of consumers should be a primary consideration. Marketing practices that exploit vulnerabilities, promote excessive consumption, or harm consumer welfare are unethical.

By adhering to ethical principles and fostering responsible marketing, businesses can build trust, cultivate loyal customer relationships, and contribute to a more transparent and consumer-centric marketplace.

Word-of-mouth marketing, social proof, and groupthink are powerful forces that shape consumer behavior in the digital age. These phenomena tap into fundamental human desires for social validation, guidance, and conformity. When harnessed ethically and responsibly, they can help businesses build trust, credibility, and customer loyalty. However, businesses must remain vigilant about the risks of manipulation, misinformation, and unethical practices. By prioritizing transparency, consumer autonomy, and responsible marketing, businesses can navigate the complexities of these social dynamics while fostering a more ethical and consumer-centric marketplace.

Brand Loyalty and Identity Psychology

Brand loyalty is a vital aspect of modern consumer behavior. It represents the inclination of customers to consistently choose and purchase products or services from a particular brand over others in the market. Understanding how consumers form brand loyalties is crucial for businesses aiming to build lasting customer relationships and secure a competitive edge. This section explores the intricate process through which consumers develop brand loyalties, examining various factors that influence this phenomenon. From the emotional connection consumers establish with brands to the role of trust, quality, and marketing strategies, this discussion dives into the psychology and behavior behind brand loyalty.

One of the primary drivers behind brand loyalty is the emotional connection that consumers develop with a brand. Brands often strive to create and maintain an emotional bond with their customers by appealing to their values, beliefs, and aspirations. When consumers feel that a brand aligns with their own identity or values, they are more likely to form a strong and lasting bond. For instance, Apple Inc. has successfully cultivated a loyal customer base by fostering a sense of innovation and creativity, making consumers feel like they are part of a community of like-minded individuals.

This emotional connection can manifest in various ways, including nostalgia, trust, and the brand's ability to evoke positive emotions. For example, people may feel nostalgic when using products from a brand they have grown up with, such as Coca-Cola. This sense of nostalgia can lead to brand loyalty, as consumers associate the brand with fond memories from their past. Moreover, trust plays a pivotal role in building emotional connections. Brands that consistently deliver on their promises and provide quality products or services are more likely to gain and maintain the trust of their customers, fostering brand loyalty over time.

Quality and consistency are fundamental factors that drive brand loyalty. Consumers often return to a brand they trust and perceive as delivering a consistent level of quality. Brands that prioritize quality assurance not only attract new customers but also retain existing ones. When consumers have positive experiences with a product or service, they are more likely to become repeat buyers and recommend the brand to others.

Brands like Honda and Toyota are renowned for their commitment to quality and consistency, which has resulted in strong brand loyalty among their customers. These companies have built their reputation on manufacturing reliable and durable vehicles, thus creating a sense of trust and loyalty among consumers who value these attributes.

Trust is a foundational element in the formation of brand loyalty. Consumers are more likely to be loyal to a brand they trust to fulfill their needs and expectations consistently. Trust can stem from a variety of factors, including product quality, ethical business practices, and reliable customer service.

Ethical considerations are becoming increasingly important for modern consumers. Brands that demonstrate social responsibility and sustainability practices often gain the trust and loyalty of consumers who prioritize these values. For instance, Patagonia has built a loyal customer base by promoting environmentally friendly practices and donating a percentage of its profits to environmental causes. Consumers who share these values are more likely to form a strong bond with the brand.

Effective marketing strategies play a pivotal role in shaping consumers' perceptions and fostering brand loyalty. Brands that invest in building awareness, creating engaging content, and establishing a strong online presence are better positioned to connect with consumers and encourage brand loyalty.

Social media has become a powerful tool for brand engagement and loyalty. Brands that interact with their customers on platforms like Facebook, Instagram, and Twitter can build a sense of community and encourage customer participation. User-generated content, such as reviews, testimonials, and posts from satisfied customers, can further strengthen brand loyalty by providing social proof of a brand's value and quality.

Loyalty programs and incentives are commonly used by brands to reward and retain their customers. These programs, which offer discounts, exclusive access, or loyalty points, can be effective in encouraging repeat purchases and maintaining customer loyalty over time. For example, Starbucks' rewards program not only encourages customers to visit their stores frequently but also fosters a sense of belonging to the Starbucks community.

A brand's ability to stand out in a competitive market and differentiate itself from competitors can significantly impact the formation of brand loyalty. Consumers often choose brands that offer unique features, benefits, or experiences that they cannot find elsewhere.

Brands that excel in innovation and differentiation tend to build stronger and more enduring loyalties. Companies like Tesla have disrupted the automotive industry by offering electric vehicles with cutting-edge technology, creating a passionate and loyal following among consumers who are drawn to their innovative approach.

Brand loyalty is a complex phenomenon influenced by a myriad of factors, including emotional connections, quality, trust, marketing strategies, and differentiation. Businesses that understand and effectively leverage these factors are better positioned to cultivate lasting relationships with their customers. By nurturing emotional bonds, consistently delivering quality, earning trust, employing engaging marketing strategies, and offering unique experiences, brands can foster brand loyalty that withstands the test of time and competition. In a world where consumer choices abound, brand loyalty remains a valuable asset that can drive long-term success and growth for businesses.

Brand identity is a powerful and multifaceted concept that significantly influences consumer choices in today's highly competitive market. A brand's identity encompasses its visual elements, messaging, values, and overall perception in the minds of consumers. This section explores the profound impact of brand identity on consumer choices, delving into how a brand's image, reputation, and alignment with consumer values can sway purchasing decisions. By understanding the intricate relationship between brand identity and consumer choices, businesses can better strategize to attract and retain customers in a crowded marketplace.

Visual elements such as logos, color schemes, and design play a crucial role in shaping brand identity. They are often the first aspects of a brand that consumers encounter and remember. The power of visual recognition cannot be understated. Iconic logos like the Nike swoosh, Apple's apple, or the McDonald's golden arches immediately evoke associations with the respective brands they represent. This recognition not only aids in brand recall but also influences consumer choices.

Consumers are more likely to choose a product or service with a familiar and visually appealing brand identity. A well-designed and memorable logo can instill trust and confidence in potential buyers. It communicates professionalism and reliability, making consumers more inclined to consider the brand's offerings. For example, a consumer browsing the aisles of a supermarket may be more likely to purchase a product with packaging featuring a recognizable and trustworthy brand logo.

A brand's messaging and the story it tells about its products or services are integral components of its identity. These elements convey the brand's values, mission, and personality to consumers. Effective messaging can resonate deeply with consumers, shaping their perception and influencing their choices.

Consumers often gravitate toward brands whose messaging aligns with their own values and aspirations. For example, a brand that emphasizes sustainability and eco-consciousness in its messaging may attract environmentally conscious consumers. This alignment of values creates a sense of connection and fosters loyalty, as consumers feel that their choices reflect their personal beliefs.

The narrative a brand weaves about its history and journey can evoke emotional responses. Brands like Coca-Cola have masterfully crafted narratives that tap into nostalgia and tradition, making consumers feel a sense of connection to the brand's heritage. This emotional connection can sway consumer choices, as individuals seek products that resonate with their own stories and experiences.

A brand's reputation is intricately tied to its identity and can heavily impact consumer choices. Consumers rely on the reputation of a brand to make informed decisions about the products or services they purchase. A positive reputation is built on a foundation of trust, consistency, and quality.

Consumers are more likely to choose a brand with a strong reputation for delivering on its promises. Brands that consistently provide high-quality products or services earn the trust of their customers, making them the go-to choice in their respective industries. This trust extends beyond the specific product to the entire brand, influencing consumers to explore other offerings within the brand's portfolio.

A tarnished reputation or negative associations can deter consumers from choosing a brand. In today's interconnected world, news of ethical violations, product recalls, or subpar customer experiences can spread rapidly and erode consumer trust. Maintaining a positive brand identity and proactively addressing any issues that may harm reputation is essential for retaining consumer loyalty.

Brand identity has the remarkable ability to forge emotional connections with consumers. Brands that successfully evoke positive emotions, whether through their messaging, storytelling, or overall image, are more likely to foster brand loyalty. An emotional connection goes beyond rational decision-making; it taps into the consumer's feelings and desires.

Brands like Disney, with their emphasis on magic, joy, and nostalgia, have a loyal following of consumers who associate the brand with cherished memories and emotions. These consumers are not merely making practical choices; they are expressing their emotional attachment to the brand through their purchases.

This emotional loyalty translates into repeat business and advocacy. Consumers who feel a strong connection to a brand are more likely to choose it consistently and recommend it to others. In essence, brand identity becomes a conduit for building relationships and creating brand evangelists who advocate for the brand organically.

In a crowded marketplace, brand identity serves as a means of differentiation and competitive advantage. Brands that establish a unique and compelling identity are better positioned to stand out and capture the attention of consumers.

A distinct brand identity can give a brand a competitive edge by highlighting what sets it apart from competitors. Whether it's a commitment to innovation, a focus on luxury, or an emphasis on affordability, a brand's identity communicates its unique value proposition to consumers. As a result, consumers looking for specific attributes in a product or service are more likely to choose the brand that aligns with their preferences.

Moreover, a strong brand identity can command premium pricing. Consumers are often willing to pay more for products or services associated with a brand they perceive as prestigious or offering superior quality. This pricing power can boost a brand's profitability and market share.

Brand identity exerts a profound influence on consumer choices, encompassing visual recognition, messaging, reputation, emotional connections, differentiation, and competitive advantage. Businesses that invest in crafting a compelling and authentic brand identity are better equipped to attract and retain customers in a competitive market. Understanding the complex interplay between brand identity and consumer choices is essential for building brand loyalty, increasing market share, and achieving long-term success in today's dynamic business landscape. By aligning their identity with consumer values and aspirations, brands can create enduring connections that drive consumer choices and foster loyalty.

Luxury and Premium Brand Psychology

L uxury and premium brands hold a unique allure in the consumer market. They go beyond functional utility and often evoke strong emotional responses from their customers. Understanding the psychology of luxury and premium brand consumers is essential for marketers and businesses looking to cater to this distinct segment of the market. This section explores the complexities of consumer psychology in the context of luxury and premium brands, exploring the underlying motivations, emotions, and behaviors that drive individuals to seek and engage with these brands.

A fundamental psychological driver behind the attraction to luxury and premium brands is the pursuit of status and social identity. These brands often serve as symbols of success and prestige, allowing consumers to communicate their social standing and aspirations to others. When individuals choose luxury or premium products, they are making a statement about their place in society.

Research in social psychology has shown that individuals often seek to belong to specific social groups or to be perceived in certain ways by their peers. Luxury and premium brands provide a means for consumers to signal their affiliation with a particular social group—whether it be an elite class, fashion-conscious community, or trendsetting cohort.

Consumers of luxury and premium brands may derive a sense of self-esteem and validation from their purchases. Owning and displaying such products can boost their self-image and reinforce their perceived social status. This phenomenon is often referred to as "conspicuous consumption," where consumers use visible luxury possessions to signal their success and attract positive attention from others.

Luxury and premium brands evoke powerful emotions that set them apart from ordinary products. The purchase and ownership of these brands are often associated with intense feelings of pleasure, pride, and happiness. The concept of the "hedonic treadmill" suggests that individuals adapt quickly to material possessions, causing the initial pleasure of acquisition to fade over time. However, luxury and premium brands tend to provide a more enduring source of hedonic satisfaction.

Psychologists have identified several emotional drivers of luxury consumption:

Eudaimonic Well-being: Luxury and premium brands are often linked to a sense of fulfillment, self-actualization, and personal growth. Consumers may perceive these products as investments in their own well-being and self-fulfillment.

Psychological Rewards: The act of acquiring luxury and premium items can stimulate the brain's reward system, releasing neurotransmitters associated with pleasure and satisfaction. This reward-driven behavior contributes to the addictive nature of luxury consumption.

Emotional Expression: Luxury and premium brands allow consumers to express their personality, tastes, and values. The emotional connection between consumers and these brands is further strengthened when the brands align with the consumers' self-concept.

Status and Power: The emotions of prestige, power, and superiority are often associated with luxury consumption. Owning these brands can lead to feelings of accomplishment and the gratification of being a member of an exclusive group.

The psychology of luxury and premium brand consumers is also influenced by the perceived quality and exclusivity associated with these products. Perceived quality goes beyond the tangible attributes of a product; it encompasses consumers' beliefs about superior craftsmanship, materials, and attention to detail. This perception of quality can create a halo effect, where consumers attribute positive qualities to the entire brand portfolio based on a single premium product.

Exclusivity plays a pivotal role in the allure of luxury and premium brands. Consumers are drawn to the idea that these brands are not accessible to everyone, creating a sense of scarcity and desirability. The limited availability of luxury products, exclusive boutiques, and invitation-only events contribute to the perception of exclusivity.

The psychology of perceived quality and exclusivity is rooted in cognitive biases such as the halo effect, confirmation bias, and scarcity heuristic. These biases shape consumers' perceptions and preferences, leading them to seek out and value luxury and premium brands more highly.

Luxury and premium brands often excel in the art of storytelling. They craft narratives that go beyond the product itself, immersing consumers in a world of aspiration, heritage, and sophistication. These narratives play a crucial role in shaping consumer identities and reinforcing their self-concept.

Consumers of luxury brands often perceive themselves as protagonists in these brand stories. For example, the story of a luxury fashion brand might center on elegance, creativity, and individuality, attracting consumers who want to embody these traits. The brand narrative becomes a mirror through which consumers see themselves, and the products serve as symbolic artifacts of that identity.

Research in psychology suggests that individuals are drawn to narratives that resonate with their self-concept and values. Luxury and premium brands leverage this insight by creating narratives that align with the aspirations and desires of their target consumers. The storytelling element not only fosters emotional connections but also fosters a sense of belonging to a community of like-minded individuals who share similar values and aspirations.

Luxury and premium brands prioritize the creation of exceptional consumer experiences that engage multiple senses. These experiences go beyond the transactional act of buying a product and often involve the physical environment, personalized service, and sensory elements such as sight, touch, and smell.

The sensory engagement associated with luxury and premium brands activates the brain's limbic system, which is responsible for emotions and memory. As a result, consumers form strong emotional associations with the brand that extend beyond the product itself.

Luxury retail stores, for example, are designed to provide an immersive and sensory-rich environment. The use of premium materials, elegant lighting, and soothing music contributes to a luxurious ambiance that complements the products on display. Similarly, luxury perfumes often focus on the olfactory experience, with carefully crafted scents that evoke specific emotions and memories.

Sensory engagement not only enhances the hedonic experience but also reinforces the emotional connection between consumers and the brand. It leaves a lasting impression in consumers' minds and contributes to their loyalty and willingness to pay a premium for the brand's products.

Understanding the psychology of luxury and premium brand consumers is essential for businesses operating in these markets. Consumers of luxury and premium brands are driven by complex motivations rooted in social identity, emotional engagement, and perceptions of quality and exclusivity. These consumers seek more than functional utility; they seek status, hedonic satisfaction, and a sense of belonging to a select group. By aligning their marketing strategies with these psychological drivers, businesses can not only attract and retain luxury consumers but also create enduring brand loyalty and positive associations that transcend product functionality. Luxury and premium brands are, in essence, purveyors of dreams and aspirations, and their success lies in their ability to fulfill these desires for their discerning consumers.

Psychology of Brand
Loyalty Programs

L oyalty programs have become a ubiquitous feature of modern consumerism. From airline frequent flyer programs to retail store memberships, these initiatives aim to incentivize repeat business by rewarding loyal customers. The effectiveness of loyalty programs has been a subject of interest and debate among businesses and researchers alike. This section explores into the world of loyalty programs, exploring their impact on consumer behavior, the factors that contribute to their effectiveness, and the potential pitfalls that businesses should be aware of.

Loyalty programs are designed to influence consumer behavior in several ways. One of the primary objectives is to encourage repeat purchases. When consumers are offered rewards, discounts, or exclusive benefits for their continued patronage, they are more likely to return to the same business. This repeated engagement can lead to increased customer lifetime value and higher revenue for the company.

Loyalty programs often promote customer retention. By fostering a sense of connection and commitment to the brand, these programs reduce the likelihood of customers switching to competitors. The promise of future rewards creates a barrier to exit, anchoring consumers to a particular business.

Beyond repeat purchases and retention, loyalty programs can also drive customer advocacy. Satisfied and loyal customers are more likely to refer friends and family to the business, leading to organic growth through word-of-mouth marketing.

The effectiveness of loyalty programs can be attributed

to various psychological mechanisms that tap into human behavior and decision-making processes. Some of these mechanisms include:

Reciprocity: The principle of reciprocity suggests that when people receive something valuable, they feel compelled to give something in return. In the context of loyalty programs, customers perceive the rewards or benefits they receive as a form of reciprocity for their continued business.

Hedonic Rewards: Loyalty programs often offer hedonic rewards, such as discounts, free products, or exclusive experiences. These rewards trigger positive emotions, enhancing the overall customer experience and reinforcing the desire to return to the business.

Status and Identity: Loyalty programs can elevate a customer's sense of status and identity. Being a member of an exclusive club or achieving a higher tier within a program can boost self-esteem and create a sense of belonging.

Loss Aversion: People tend to be averse to losing what they have already gained. Loyalty program members may fear losing out on accumulated rewards if they switch to a competitor, further cementing their loyalty.

Anchoring: Loyalty programs often anchor customers to the business by setting a reference point for comparison. Once customers have received rewards or achieved a certain status within a program, they may be reluctant to forgo those benefits by switching to a different brand.

The effectiveness of loyalty programs can vary depending on several factors:

Program Design: Well-designed programs with clear and attainable rewards tend to be more effective. Customers should easily understand the value they can derive from participating.

Customer Segmentation: Tailoring loyalty programs to specific customer segments can enhance their impact. Different groups of customers may respond differently to various incentives.

Communication and Engagement: Regular communication with program members and opportunities for engagement, such as personalized offers and promotions, can keep customers actively participating in the program.

Technology and Data: Leveraging technology and data analytics allows businesses to track customer behavior and preferences, enabling them to offer highly targeted rewards and incentives.

Competitive Landscape: The competitive environment in a particular industry can affect the effectiveness of a loyalty program. If competitors offer similar programs, businesses may need to differentiate theirs to stand out.

Simplicity and Accessibility: Loyalty programs should be easy to understand and participate in. Complex rules or high barriers to entry can deter potential members.

Consistency and Longevity: The long-term effectiveness of loyalty programs often depends on their consistency and longevity. Programs that are abruptly discontinued can erode customer trust.

While loyalty programs can be highly effective, they are not without challenges and potential pitfalls:

Costs: Offering rewards and benefits can be costly, and businesses must carefully manage the financial aspect of loyalty programs to ensure they remain sustainable.

Customer Expectations: Over time, customers may come to expect ever-increasing rewards, leading to escalating program costs and diminishing returns on investment.

Customer Saturation: In some industries, customers may become oversaturated with loyalty program options, making it challenging for any single program to stand out.

Data Privacy Concerns: Collecting and analyzing customer data for personalization can raise privacy concerns, and businesses must navigate this issue transparently and responsibly.

Lack of Differentiation: Loyalty programs that offer generic rewards or fail to distinguish themselves from competitors may struggle to attract and retain members.

Measuring the effectiveness of loyalty programs is crucial for businesses to assess their return on investment (ROI). Some key performance indicators (KPIs) and metrics for evaluating program effectiveness include:

Customer Retention Rate: The percentage of customers who continue to do business with the company over time.

Customer Churn Rate: The rate at which customers discontinue their relationship with the company.

Average Purchase Frequency: How often, on average, loyalty program members make purchases.

Average Transaction Value: The average amount spent per transaction by loyalty program members.

Customer Lifetime Value: The total value a customer brings to the company over the course of their relationship.

Net Promoter Score (NPS): A measure of customer satisfaction and loyalty, often obtained through surveys or feedback mechanisms within the loyalty program.

Cost of Customer Acquisition: Understanding how much it costs to acquire and retain customers through the loyalty program compared to other marketing strategies.

Redemption Rates: Tracking how often customers redeem rewards and incentives, providing insights into the program's engagement level.

Referral Rates: Measuring the extent to which loyal customers refer new customers to the business, indicating the program's impact on customer advocacy.

Customer Segmentation: Analyzing the behavior and preferences of different customer segments within the loyalty program to tailor offerings effectively.

ROI: Calculating the return on investment by comparing the program's costs to the increased revenue generated from loyal customers.

Effective measurement and analysis of these metrics can help businesses fine-tune their loyalty programs, optimize their strategies, and ensure that the programs continue to deliver value both to customers and the company's bottom line.

The effectiveness of loyalty programs in influencing consumer behavior, fostering brand loyalty, and driving revenue is well-established. These programs tap into psychological mechanisms such as reciprocity, hedonic rewards, and status to incentivize repeat business and customer retention. However, their success depends on several factors, including program design, customer segmentation, communication, and the competitive landscape.

While loyalty programs can be powerful tools for businesses, they are not without challenges, including the cost of rewards, customer expectations, and data privacy concerns. To ensure long-term success, businesses must carefully manage and measure the effectiveness of their loyalty programs, considering key performance indicators and metrics.

In an ever-competitive market where customer loyalty is highly sought after, loyalty programs offer a strategic advantage. When designed thoughtfully and executed effectively, they not only drive revenue but also strengthen the emotional connection between businesses and their customers, fostering a sense of commitment and reciprocity that goes beyond transactional interactions.

The foundation of a successful loyalty program lies in a deep understanding of your customers' needs, preferences, and behaviors. Before creating a program, conduct comprehensive market research, collect customer data, and analyze customer feedback. This information will help you tailor the program to meet the specific desires of your target audience.

Demographics: What are the age, gender, location, and income levels of your customers? These demographics can influence the types of rewards and incentives that resonate with them.

Purchase History: Analyze what customers have bought in the past to identify patterns and preferences. This can inform the types of rewards or product recommendations you offer.

Communication Channels: Determine the preferred communication channels of your customers. Some may prefer email, while others may prefer mobile apps or social media.

Feedback and Surveys: Regularly seek feedback from your customers to understand their evolving needs and preferences. Surveys and feedback mechanisms within the loyalty program can provide valuable insights.

Successful loyalty programs are rooted in a customer-centric approach, ensuring that the program is not only attractive but also relevant to the target audience.

The rewards structure of your loyalty program should be transparent, easy to understand, and attainable. Ambiguity or complexity can deter participation and frustrate customers. Therefore, it's crucial to:

Clearly outline the benefits: Communicate the specific rewards, discounts, or benefits that customers can earn by participating in the program. Use simple, straightforward language to describe these benefits.

Set achievable milestones: Define how customers can earn points or rewards and establish achievable milestones. For example, a coffee shop loyalty program might offer a free coffee after every ten purchases.

Offer immediate gratification: Consider providing instant

rewards or benefits to encourage immediate participation and engagement.

Include tiered levels: Some loyalty programs have tiered structures, offering increasing rewards as customers reach higher levels. This can motivate customers to strive for elite status.

When customers can easily grasp the value they will receive and the effort required to earn rewards, they are more likely to engage and stay committed to the program.

Personalization is a key driver of loyalty program success. Tailoring your communications and rewards to individual customer preferences enhances the customer experience and fosters a sense of special treatment. To achieve personalization:

Leverage customer data: Use customer data to create personalized recommendations, offers, and rewards. For example, an e-commerce loyalty program might recommend products based on a customer's past purchases.

Segment your audience: Divide your loyalty program members into distinct segments based on factors like purchase history, demographics, or behavior. This allows for more targeted and relevant communication.

Behavioral triggers: Set up automated triggers that send personalized messages or offers based on customer actions or milestones within the program. For instance, a fitness app might send a discount on workout gear when a customer achieves a fitness goal.

Multichannel engagement: Engage with customers through their preferred channels, whether it's email, mobile apps, SMS, or social media. Ensure that the content and timing of your communications align with their preferences.

Personalized experiences make customers feel valued and understood, strengthening their emotional connection to your brand and loyalty program.

The success of loyalty programs often hinges on user-friendly technology and mobile accessibility. Many customers prefer the convenience of managing their loyalty rewards via mobile apps or websites. Therefore, consider the following:

Mobile apps: Create a dedicated mobile app for your loyalty program, allowing customers to track their progress, redeem rewards, and receive personalized notifications.

Mobile payments: If applicable, integrate mobile payment options into your loyalty program to streamline transactions and enhance convenience.

Seamless online and offline integration: Ensure that your loyalty program works seamlessly across both online and offline channels. Customers should be able to earn and redeem rewards whether they shop in-store, online, or through a mobile app.

Data security: Prioritize the security of customer data, especially in the case of mobile apps that may store sensitive information. Implement robust data encryption and protection measures.

Accessibility and ease of use: Test the user interface and experience of your loyalty program's digital components to ensure they are intuitive and accessible to all customers.

A mobile-friendly and technologically advanced loyalty program can significantly enhance customer engagement and retention, particularly among tech-savvy consumers.

The success of a loyalty program relies on consistent and engaging communication with members. Develop a communication strategy that includes:

Welcome emails: Send a warm welcome email to new members, introducing them to the program and its benefits.

Periodic updates: Keep members informed about their progress, rewards earned, and upcoming promotions. Regularly remind them of the value of participating.

Exclusive offers: Offer members exclusive promotions, discounts, or early access to new products or services. Create a sense of exclusivity and privilege.

Special occasions: Recognize and celebrate milestones such as birthdays or program anniversaries with personalized messages or rewards.

Feedback mechanisms: Encourage members to provide feedback and suggestions, showing that you value their input and are committed to improvement.

Re-engagement campaigns: Identify inactive members and implement re-engagement campaigns to reignite their interest in the program.

Effective and engaging communication keeps members connected to the program and motivated to continue their participation.

Creating a successful loyalty program that engages and retains customers is a multifaceted endeavor that requires a deep understanding of customer needs, clear and attainable rewards structures, personalized experiences, user-friendly technology, and consistent communication. A well-designed loyalty program can drive repeat business, foster brand loyalty, and contribute to long-term customer relationships.

Businesses that invest in creating customer-centric loyalty programs stand to benefit not only from increased customer retention and loyalty but also from valuable insights gained through customer data and feedback. As customer expectations continue to evolve, staying attuned to their needs and preferences is essential for the ongoing success of loyalty initiatives. Ultimately, a successful loyalty program is a win-win for both businesses and their valued customers.

The Psychology Behind Free Trials and Samples

Free trials and samples have become ubiquitous in the world of marketing, drawing consumers in with the promise of something for nothing. This marketing strategy taps into the psychology of consumers in a powerful way, capitalizing on a range of psychological principles to influence behavior. Understanding the psychology behind free trials and samples can shed light on why consumers are drawn to these offers, how they affect decision-making, and their implications for both businesses and individuals.

One of the foundational principles behind the psychology of free trials and samples is the principle of reciprocity. This principle suggests that when someone receives something for free or a favor from another person, they often feel a natural inclination to reciprocate. When businesses offer free trials or samples, they are essentially giving consumers a taste of their product or service, creating a sense of indebtedness. This psychological dynamic can lead consumers to be more inclined to make a purchase in return for the freebie, as they seek to balance the scales of reciprocity.

Free trials and samples also work by reducing the perceived risk associated with a purchase. When consumers can try a product or service without a financial commitment, it lowers the psychological barrier to trying something new. This is especially powerful when dealing with products or services that consumers may be hesitant to try due to uncertainty about their quality or effectiveness. By allowing consumers to experience a product firsthand, businesses aim to mitigate doubts and hesitations, making it easier for consumers to take the plunge and make a purchase.

The endowment effect is another psychological phenomenon that plays a role in the effectiveness of free trials and samples. It suggests that people tend to ascribe more value to things they own or possess. When consumers receive a free sample or trial of a product, they temporarily possess it, even if it's just for a short period. This sense of ownership can lead individuals to overvalue the product and develop a stronger attachment to it. Consequently, when the trial period ends, consumers may be more inclined to purchase the full product to maintain their sense of ownership and the perceived value they've assigned to it.

Free trials and samples can also capitalize on the psychology of decision delay. When consumers are faced with making a purchase decision, they often experience a sense of cognitive dissonance and uncertainty. Offering a free trial or sample allows consumers to delay the final purchase decision while still satisfying their curiosity and immediate needs. This delay can provide a valuable window of opportunity for businesses to nurture leads, build trust, and provide additional information or incentives that can ultimately lead to a conversion. In essence, free trials and samples serve as a way to engage consumers and keep them in the decision-making process for a longer duration, increasing the likelihood of a positive outcome for both parties involved.

In conclusion, the psychology of free trials and samples is a complex interplay of reciprocity, risk reduction, the endowment effect, and decision delay. By understanding these psychological principles, businesses can craft more effective marketing strategies and consumers can become more aware of the underlying motivations that drive their choices. While free trials and samples can be powerful tools for both consumers and businesses, it's essential for individuals to exercise discernment and evaluate whether the value offered truly aligns with their needs and preferences, rather than succumbing to the allure of something for nothing.

Navigating the Consumer Maze: The Psychology Behind Retail Speed Bumps

R etail stores are more than just places to shop; they are carefully designed environments where psychology plays a pivotal role in influencing consumer behavior. One fascinating aspect of retail psychology is the incorporation of "speed bumps" within the store layout. These speed bumps are strategic design elements or tactics used to slow down shoppers, capturing their attention and encouraging specific behaviors. In this exploration, we will delve into the psychology behind these retail speed bumps, understanding how they work and why they are essential for both retailers and consumers.

The primary purpose of retail speed bumps is to interrupt the flow of shoppers, diverting their attention and encouraging them to engage with products or store features. These interruptions are carefully designed to serve various goals. For instance, end-cap displays, which are shelves or promotional setups at the end of aisles, act as speed bumps by creating a visual barrier. They disrupt the natural walking path, compelling customers to stop and explore the featured products. This tactic can boost sales of specific items and create a more dynamic shopping experience.

Another common type of retail speed bump is the "power aisle." This is a designated aisle with high-visibility displays of featured products. Placing such an aisle perpendicular to the shopper's natural path can slow them down and lead to more spontaneous purchases. These tactics demonstrate how retailers use psychology to guide consumer behavior.

Understanding the psychology behind retail speed bumps involves delving into various cognitive and emotional mechanisms. One critical aspect is attention. Speed bumps divert attention away from the primary goal of moving quickly through the store, focusing it instead on the featured products or displays. This redirection of attention can trigger curiosity and interest in the shopper, potentially leading to impulse purchases or deeper exploration.

Emotion also plays a significant role. Speed bumps often incorporate elements that evoke emotions, such as color schemes, lighting, or sensory experiences. For example, soft lighting and soothing music can create a calming atmosphere, encouraging shoppers to linger and browse. On the other hand, vibrant colors and bold signage can generate excitement and urgency, prompting consumers to take action.

The psychology of retail speed bumps has a profound impact on consumer behavior. It can lead to increased sales, extended shopping times, and enhanced customer satisfaction. When shoppers are slowed down and engaged, they are more likely to discover new products, make impulse purchases, and feel more positive about their shopping experience.

Speed bumps can also create a sense of exploration and discovery, transforming the shopping trip into a more immersive and enjoyable activity. Consumers may find themselves browsing longer, which can lead to higher spending. For retailers, this translates into increased revenue and improved brand loyalty.

In conclusion, the psychology of speed bumps in retail stores is a powerful tool that influences consumer behavior in subtle yet significant ways. By strategically placing interruptions within the shopping environment, retailers can capture attention, stimulate emotions, and ultimately drive sales. While some may perceive these tactics as manipulative, they are a fundamental part of the retail industry, benefiting both businesses and consumers. Understanding the psychology behind retail speed bumps provides valuable insights into the complex relationship between retail design and human behavior, shedding light on the art and science of shopping. As consumers, being aware of these tactics can help us make more informed choices and navigate the retail landscape with a deeper understanding of the forces at play.

Unpacking the Psychology
of Shopping Cart Size

The shopping cart, a seemingly mundane tool in the retail world, plays a surprisingly significant role in shaping our shopping experiences. Beyond its utilitarian function of carrying groceries and products, the size of a shopping cart has a profound impact on our behavior as consumers. In this section, we traverse into the psychology of shopping cart size, dissecting how this seemingly simple factor can influence the way we shop, our purchasing decisions, and even our perceptions of value.

The size of a shopping cart is not arbitrary; it's a carefully designed feature meant to encourage specific consumer behaviors. Retailers understand that the cart size influences how much shoppers buy. Larger carts can lead to over-purchasing, as shoppers are more likely to fill them with items they hadn't initially planned to buy. This phenomenon, known as the "shopping cart illusion," occurs because the cart's size creates a psychological gap between the number of items placed inside and the perception of space remaining. As a result, consumers often buy more than they need, contributing to increased sales for the retailer.

Smaller shopping carts can have the opposite effect. They encourage shoppers to be more selective and mindful of their purchases, leading to reduced spending. Smaller carts may also subtly convey scarcity, creating a sense of urgency that prompts consumers to make quicker decisions. This deliberate manipulation of cart size is a testament to the intricate psychology at play in retail environments.

The size of a shopping cart not only affects the quantity of items purchased but also influences consumers' perceptions of value. When shoppers see their selections occupying a larger space within the cart, they may feel a sense of accomplishment, believing they are getting more for their money. This perception of abundance can lead to increased customer satisfaction and loyalty, as customers associate the store with a good deal.

On the contrary, smaller carts may make consumers more conscious of space limitations. As the cart fills up quickly, shoppers might become more aware of their spending, potentially leading to feelings of constraint or frustration. Retailers often leverage this psychological effect when offering discounts or promotions, as it can encourage customers to make additional purchases to fill the cart and maximize their perceived value.

Beyond the immediate shopping trip, the size of a shopping cart can also impact long-term shopping habits. Larger carts, by encouraging over-purchasing, may lead to food waste and increased expenses for consumers. On the other hand, smaller carts promote more mindful shopping, potentially reducing waste and promoting healthier, budget-conscious choices.

Cart size can influence shopping efficiency. Shoppers with larger carts may spend more time navigating the store, searching for items to fill the empty space. Smaller cart users, in contrast, tend to complete their shopping more quickly and efficiently. Retailers consider these factors when deciding on cart sizes, as they can affect store traffic flow and the overall shopping experience.

In conclusion, the psychology of shopping cart size serves as a fascinating example of how subtle design elements can significantly influence consumer behavior and perceptions. The careful consideration of cart size by retailers illustrates their understanding of human psychology and their ability to use it to their advantage. Shoppers should be aware of these psychological effects to make more informed choices when navigating the retail landscape. Whether large or small, the shopping cart size is far from arbitrary; it is a powerful tool that shapes our shopping experiences, influences our spending habits, and even affects our perceptions of value. Understanding these dynamics empowers consumers to make more mindful decisions and navigate the world of retail with greater insight.

Advertising and Persuasion

Persuasive advertising is an art form that harnesses the power of psychology to influence consumer behavior. In today's saturated marketplace, businesses need to not only capture consumers' attention but also convince them to make purchasing decisions. This section explores the intricate psychological principles that underlie persuasive advertising. By understanding the workings of the human mind, marketers can craft compelling advertisements that resonate with their target audience, drive sales, and build brand loyalty.

One of the fundamental psychological principles behind persuasive advertising is the use of emotional appeal. Emotions play a significant role in decision-making, often overshadowing rational thought processes. Effective advertising taps into these emotions to create a connection between the consumer and the product or service being promoted.

Advertisers often use a range of emotional triggers, such as happiness, fear, nostalgia, or empathy, to elicit specific feelings in the audience. For example, a heartwarming commercial featuring a family reunion may evoke feelings of nostalgia and happiness, associating those emotions with the advertised product or brand. Conversely, a public service announcement about the dangers of smoking may use fear as an emotional lever to discourage a particular behavior.

The key to success in using emotional appeal lies in understanding the target audience's needs, desires, and pain points. By aligning the emotional content of an advertisement with the audience's emotional state, advertisers can effectively capture attention and persuade viewers to take action.

Psychological principles like social proof and conformity play a significant role in persuasive advertising. Social proof is the tendency for people to follow the actions and behaviors of others when they are uncertain about what to do. In advertising, this principle is leveraged by showcasing testimonials, user reviews, and endorsements from celebrities or experts.

Online retailers often display user ratings and reviews alongside products, allowing potential buyers to see how many others have purchased and positively reviewed the product. This social proof reassures consumers about the product's quality and popularity, making them more likely to make a purchase.

Conformity, on the other hand, is the inclination to align one's behavior with the perceived norms of a group. Advertisements often depict scenarios where individuals or groups are seen using and enjoying the advertised product. This portrayal encourages viewers to conform to the idea that using the product is a normal and desirable behavior.

Scarcity is a psychological principle that exploits people's fear of missing out (FOMO). When consumers perceive a product or opportunity as scarce or limited in availability, it triggers a sense of urgency and desire to acquire it before it runs out.

Persuasive advertising frequently employs tactics that emphasize scarcity, such as countdown timers, limited-time offers, or statements like "only a few items left in stock." These techniques play on consumers' fear of missing out on a valuable opportunity, driving them to make quick purchasing decisions.

FOMO is heightened through the use of social media and influencer marketing. Consumers see their peers or favorite influencers using or endorsing a product, creating a sense of urgency to be part of the same experience.

Cognitive biases are systematic patterns of deviation from norm or rationality in judgment. In the context of advertising, certain cognitive biases can be harnessed to persuade consumers. One such bias is anchoring, where people rely heavily on the first piece of information they encounter when making decisions.

Advertisers often use anchoring by presenting a higher-priced product first and then offering a lower-priced alternative. The initial high price "anchors" the consumer's perception of value, making the lower price seem like a bargain. For example, a furniture store might display a premium sofa set with a high price tag before presenting a more affordable option, making the latter appear more appealing and affordable by comparison.

Another cognitive bias frequently used in advertising is the availability heuristic. This bias leads people to overestimate the likelihood of events based on their availability in memory. Advertisers leverage this bias by emphasizing the prevalence and popularity of their product. Claims like "the best-selling brand" or "trusted by millions" capitalize on the availability heuristic, making consumers more likely to choose the advertised product due to its perceived popularity and trustworthiness.

The narrative effect is a psychological principle that underscores the power of storytelling in persuasive advertising. Human brains are wired to respond to stories and narratives, as they engage emotions, capture attention, and are more memorable than straightforward information.

Effective advertising often incorporates storytelling to create a connection between the consumer and the brand. Narratives can take various forms, from emotional customer testimonials to compelling origin stories of the brand itself. By weaving a narrative, advertisers not only convey information but also evoke emotions, making the message more persuasive and memorable.

A car advertisement may tell the story of a family's road trip adventure, emphasizing the safety features and reliability of the vehicle. This narrative approach helps consumers envision themselves in a similar scenario, making the advertised car more appealing as it becomes a part of their own story.

Persuasive advertising relies on a deep understanding of psychological principles to influence consumer choices effectively. By leveraging emotional appeal, social proof, scarcity, cognitive biases, and storytelling, advertisers can create compelling messages that resonate with their target audience. In a world inundated with advertisements, those that tap into these psychological triggers stand out, drive consumer behavior, and ultimately contribute to the success of brands and products in the marketplace. Understanding and applying these psychological principles is essential for advertisers seeking to create persuasive campaigns that connect with consumers on a profound level.

Creating an effective advertising campaign is both an art and a science. In today's competitive marketplace, businesses must capture the attention of their target audience and deliver compelling messages that drive action. This section explores techniques that marketers and advertisers use to craft successful ad campaigns. From understanding the audience and setting clear objectives to leveraging creativity and utilizing data-driven insights, these techniques serve as the foundation for creating campaigns that resonate with consumers and achieve desired results.

One of the cornerstones of a successful ad campaign is a deep understanding of the target audience. Marketers must go beyond surface-level demographics to grasp the psychographics, behaviors, and preferences of their potential customers. Effective campaigns are tailored to resonate with specific audience segments, addressing their unique needs and desires.

Audience segmentation involves dividing the target market into distinct groups based on shared characteristics. These segments could be defined by factors such as age, gender, income, lifestyle, or purchasing behavior. For example, an athletic footwear brand may segment its audience into categories like professional athletes, fitness enthusiasts, and casual joggers.

Once segments are identified, advertisers can create personalized messages that speak directly to each group's interests and motivations. This approach not only increases the relevance of the campaign but also enhances the likelihood of capturing the attention and engagement of the intended audience.

Effective ad campaigns begin with clearly defined and measurable objectives. Without a roadmap outlining what the campaign aims to achieve, it's challenging to assess its success or optimize performance. Objectives should be specific, measurable, achievable, relevant, and time-bound (SMART).

Common advertising objectives include increasing brand awareness, driving website traffic, generating leads, boosting sales, or improving brand loyalty. For instance, an e-commerce company launching a new product might set an objective to achieve a 20% increase in online sales within three months of the campaign's launch.

Measuring campaign success requires the use of key performance indicators (KPIs). These could include metrics like click-through rates (CTR), conversion rates, return on investment (ROI), or customer acquisition costs. Advertisers should regularly monitor these metrics throughout the campaign to assess performance and make data-driven adjustments as needed.

The art of storytelling is a powerful technique in advertising. Effective ad campaigns tell a compelling story that resonates with the audience on an emotional level. Stories have the ability to captivate, engage, and persuade, making them an invaluable tool in advertising.

One approach to creative storytelling is the use of narrative arcs. These arcs typically include elements like an introduction, conflict or problem, resolution, and a call to action. By structuring an ad campaign in this way, advertisers can take their audience on a journey that sparks curiosity, triggers emotions, and ultimately leads to action.

Crafting a clear and memorable message is essential. The message should communicate the campaign's value proposition succinctly and distinctly. The "Unique Selling Proposition" (USP) technique highlights what sets the product or service apart from competitors, giving consumers a compelling reason to choose it.

Effective ad campaigns often span multiple channels and platforms to reach consumers where they are most active. This approach, known as multi-channel marketing, ensures that the campaign message is consistently delivered across various touchpoints.

Multi-channel integration involves selecting the appropriate mix of channels, such as social media, email marketing, display advertising, search engine marketing (SEM), television, radio, and print media, among others. Each channel serves a specific purpose in the campaign, and they work together to reinforce the message.

A retail brand may launch a holiday campaign that incorporates social media posts showcasing festive products, email newsletters offering exclusive discounts, and display ads featuring holiday-themed visuals. This cohesive approach increases brand visibility and engagement while maximizing the campaign's reach.

Data-driven insights are a vital component of creating effective ad campaigns. Advertisers have access to an abundance of data that can inform decision-making, from consumer behavior to campaign performance metrics. Leveraging data enables advertisers to optimize campaigns in real-time and make informed adjustments to maximize results.

A/B testing is a common technique used to optimize ad campaigns. It involves creating multiple variations of an ad

(A and B), each with slight differences, and then measuring their performance to determine which version performs better. Elements like headlines, images, calls to action, and ad copy can be tested to identify the most effective combinations.

Analytics tools and platforms allow advertisers to track user interactions with ads, providing valuable insights into audience behavior. For example, tracking user engagement on a website landing page can reveal which elements of the page are most effective in converting visitors into customers. This information can then be used to refine the landing page and improve conversion rates.

Creating effective ad campaigns is a multifaceted endeavor that requires a deep understanding of the target audience, clear objectives, creative storytelling, multi-channel integration, and data-driven optimization. By applying these techniques, advertisers can develop campaigns that not only capture the attention of their audience but also resonate with them on a personal level. In an ever-evolving advertising landscape, staying attuned to consumer preferences and leveraging innovative strategies is essential for achieving campaign success and driving business growth. Advertisers who master these techniques are better equipped to create campaigns that deliver impactful results and build lasting connections with their audience.

Consumer Decision-Making Models

U nderstanding how consumers make decisions is crucial for businesses seeking to create effective marketing strategies and engage with their target audience. Decision-making models provide a framework for comprehending the intricate process through which consumers move from recognizing a need to making a purchase. One widely recognized model is the Consumer Decision Journey (CDJ), which maps out the stages consumers go through during their decision-making process. In this section, we will explore the CDJ and other key decision-making models, shedding light on the stages, factors, and dynamics that influence consumer choices.

The Consumer Decision Journey, also known as the customer journey or decision-making journey, is a widely used model that describes the stages consumers go through when making a purchasing decision. Originally introduced by McKinsey & Company, the CDJ comprises four key stages:

Consider: This is the initial stage where consumers recognize a need or problem. They begin searching for information and potential solutions. In the digital age, this often starts with online research. At this initial stage, businesses should focus on creating awareness and capturing consumers' attention. Content marketing, search engine optimization (SEO), and social media advertising can be effective strategies to ensure that potential customers find information about products or services when they start considering their options.

Evaluate: In this stage, consumers actively seek out information about available options. They compare brands, products, and services, relying on online reviews, recommendations, and peer opinions. During this phase, consumers actively seek information and compare products or services. To influence their choices, businesses should provide detailed and trustworthy content, including product descriptions, reviews, and expert opinions. Encouraging user-generated content and testimonials can build credibility.

Buy: The Buy stage represents the point at which consumers make their purchasing decision. They select a product or service and complete the transaction. To facilitate the purchase decision, businesses should ensure a seamless and user-friendly online shopping experience. Clear product listings, pricing transparency, and an easy-to-navigate checkout process are crucial. Additionally, offering incentives like discounts or free shipping can motivate consumers to complete their purchases.

Advocate: After the purchase, some consumers become advocates for the brand. They share positive experiences, write reviews, and recommend the product or service to others, contributing to word-of-mouth marketing. After a successful purchase, businesses can encourage customers to become advocates by providing exceptional post-purchase experiences. This may involve seeking feedback, offering loyalty programs, or creating opportunities for customers to share their positive experiences on social media or review platforms.

The CDJ is not strictly linear, as consumers can revisit stages, such as Consider or Evaluate, depending on their needs and experiences. It acknowledges the dynamic nature of consumer decision-making in the digital age, where access to information is abundant, and consumer choices are influenced by a variety of touchpoints and interactions. Continuous engagement throughout the CDJ is essential. Marketing automation tools, personalized recommendations, and targeted email campaigns can keep consumers engaged and guide them through each stage of the journey.

The AIDA model, which stands for Attention, Interest, Desire, and Action, is a classic marketing framework that predates the digital era. It describes the stages a consumer goes through when exposed to advertising or marketing messages:

Attention: Attracting the consumer's attention is the first step. Effective marketing materials must capture their interest and make them aware of the product or service. To capture consumers' attention, businesses should use eye-catching visuals, compelling headlines, and engaging content in their advertisements. Social media advertising, display ads, and influencer partnerships can be effective in generating initial interest.

Interest: Once attention is secured, the goal is to generate interest. Marketers provide information and benefits to pique the consumer's curiosity. Once attention is secured, businesses must sustain and deepen consumers' interest. This can be achieved through informative blog posts, videos, or interactive content that highlights the benefits and features of products or services.

Desire: After generating interest, marketers aim to create desire or a sense of need for the product or service. They highlight its unique selling points and advantages. To stimulate desire, marketing efforts should focus on showcasing the unique value proposition and benefits of a product or service. Testimonials, case studies, and customer success stories can demonstrate the positive impact on previous customers.

Action: The final stage is to prompt action, which can be a purchase, sign-up, or any desired behavior. The goal is to convert the consumer's interest and desire into a tangible action. The ultimate goal of any marketing strategy is to prompt action, whether it's making a purchase, signing up for a newsletter, or requesting more information. Clear and persuasive calls-to-action (CTAs) play a vital role in guiding consumers toward the desired action.

The AIDA model is widely used in advertising and has been adapted and expanded upon to accommodate the evolving landscape of consumer decision-making, particularly in the digital realm. By structuring marketing campaigns according to the AIDA model, businesses can create a logical and effective path for consumers, making it more likely that they will move through the stages to take action.

The EKB model, developed by Robert J. Lavidge and Gary A. Steiner, is another classic model used to understand consumer decision-making. EKB stands for Experiential, Knowledge-based, and Behavioral:

Experiential: The Experiential stage represents the emotional and sensory aspects of decision-making. Consumers rely on their feelings, emotions, and personal experiences to guide their choices. Marketing strategies should aim to create positive emotional experiences. Storytelling, emotional branding, and user-generated content can help connect consumers emotionally to a brand or product.

Knowledge-based: In this stage, consumers gather information and knowledge about the available options. They may research products, read reviews, and seek out expert opinions. Providing comprehensive and accurate information is essential to facilitate informed decision-making. Educational content, product guides, and frequently asked questions (FAQs) can help consumers acquire the knowledge they need.

Behavioral: The Behavioral stage is where consumers take action based on their experiences and knowledge. This can involve making a purchase, recommending a product, or taking other actions. To drive behavioral change, businesses should use persuasive techniques such as limited-time offers, discounts, or loyalty programs. Behavioral nudges and incentives can encourage consumers to take action, whether it's making a purchase or sharing their experiences.

The EKB model emphasizes the importance of both emotional and cognitive factors in consumer decision-making. It recognizes that decisions are not solely rational but also influenced by subjective experiences and feelings. The EKB model reminds businesses that consumers' decisions are not solely rational but also influenced by their emotional experiences and feelings. Effective marketing strategies should address both aspects.

The Zero Moment of Truth, coined by Google, refers to the moment when a consumer turns to the internet to research and gather information about a product or service before making a purchase decision. It acknowledges the profound impact of online resources, reviews, and social media on consumer choices.

ZMOT highlights the critical role that online presence, content, and search engine visibility play in influencing consumer decisions. It signifies the shift from traditional advertising and marketing methods to digital strategies that cater to consumers' informational needs during the decision-making process.

Online Presence: To align with ZMOT, businesses should ensure that they have a strong online presence, including a user-friendly website, active social media profiles, and positive reviews on relevant platforms. This establishes trust and credibility in the online space.

Content Marketing: Content is pivotal in the ZMOT framework. Creating informative and engaging content that answers consumers' questions and addresses their needs is essential. Blog posts, videos, infographics, and product comparisons can all serve as valuable resources during the ZMOT.

SEO and SEM: Search engine optimization (SEO) and search engine marketing (SEM) strategies are vital for ensuring that consumers find a business's content when conducting online research. Effective keyword research and optimization can enhance visibility during the ZMOT.

Online Reputation Management: Monitoring online reviews and feedback is crucial for managing a positive online reputation.

Responding to customer reviews and addressing concerns promptly can positively impact the ZMOT.

By actively participating in the Zero Moment of Truth, businesses can position themselves favorably in consumers' online research processes, increasing the likelihood of being chosen when the purchase decision is made.

Geert Hofstede's Cultural Dimensions theory explores how cultural factors can influence consumer behavior and decision-making. Hofstede identified several dimensions, including Individualism vs. Collectivism, Power Distance, Masculinity vs. Femininity, Uncertainty Avoidance, and Long-Term vs. Short-Term Orientation.

Cultural Sensitivity: Businesses should conduct cultural research to understand the cultural values, norms, and preferences of their target markets. This knowledge can inform marketing content, messaging, and imagery to resonate with specific cultural groups.

Language and Communication: Tailoring language and communication styles to align with cultural preferences is essential. This includes using appropriate idioms, avoiding cultural taboos, and considering the context in which messages are delivered.

Localization: Localization of marketing materials, including websites, advertisements, and product descriptions, is critical. It ensures that content is culturally relevant and resonates with the target audience.

Respect for Cultural Diversity: Businesses should foster an inclusive and respectful approach to cultural diversity. Embracing cultural diversity in marketing campaigns can send a positive message of inclusivity and respect.

By recognizing the influence of cultural dimensions on consumer behavior, businesses can develop marketing strategies that are sensitive to cultural nuances, avoiding cultural missteps and building stronger connections with diverse audiences.

These dimensions help explain how cultural values, norms, and preferences can impact consumer choices. For example, cultures with a high Uncertainty Avoidance dimension may prefer established and trusted brands, while those with a lower Power Distance dimension may prioritize individual decision-making over group consensus.

Consumer decision-making is a complex and multifaceted process influenced by various models and frameworks. The Consumer Decision Journey (CDJ) is a prominent model that reflects the dynamic nature of modern decision-making in the digital age. However, other models, such as the AIDA model, EKB model, Zero Moment of Truth (ZMOT), and Hofstede's Cultural Dimensions, offer valuable insights into different aspects of consumer behavior and the factors that drive their choices. In an era of abundant information and digital connectivity, businesses must not only understand these decision-making models but also adapt their marketing strategies to align with the evolving needs and preferences of consumers. By doing so, they can engage with their target audience effectively, build trust, and ultimately drive success in the marketplace.

The Psychology Behind
Free Shipping

I n today's e-commerce-driven world, online shopping has become an integral part of our daily lives. With the convenience of browsing a vast array of products and making purchases from the comfort of our homes, it's no wonder that online retailers continually seek ways to entice consumers. One of the most effective strategies employed by these retailers is the offering of free shipping. While it may seem like a simple perk, the psychology behind free shipping runs deep. In this article, we will delve into the psychological aspects of free shipping, exploring why it captivates consumers, influences their buying decisions, and ultimately drives business success.

One of the most compelling aspects of free shipping is the perceived value it offers to consumers. When shoppers encounter a product with a price tag that includes free shipping, they often view it as a more favorable deal compared to a similar product with a lower base price but additional shipping fees. This perception taps into the concept of anchoring in psychology, where the first piece of information a person receives serves as an anchor for their decision-making process. In this case, the anchor is the total price, and the inclusion of free shipping makes it more appealing.

Retailers understand this psychological phenomenon and strategically employ it to attract customers. By bundling shipping costs into the product price, they can create a perception of added value and encourage consumers to make a purchase. In essence, free shipping becomes a powerful tool to increase the perceived worth of a product, making it more likely that shoppers will click "add to cart."

The psychology of free shipping extends beyond its impact on perceived value; it also addresses a significant psychological hurdle in the online shopping process: the checkout process itself. Studies have shown that customers often abandon their shopping carts during the checkout process, primarily due to unexpected shipping costs. These additional fees disrupt the customer's sense of convenience and value, leading to frustration and cart abandonment.

Free shipping addresses this issue by eliminating the uncertainty of extra costs at checkout. When customers know from the outset that their order comes with free shipping, they are more likely to proceed confidently through the buying process. This reduction in friction leads to a higher conversion rate for online retailers. In essence, free shipping acts as a psychological bridge, helping customers traverse the final step toward completing their purchase.

Human psychology is heavily influenced by the pursuit of rewards and the avoidance of losses. Free shipping taps into this aspect of our psychology by framing the act of making a purchase as a rewarding experience. When customers are presented with the opportunity to enjoy free shipping, they perceive it as a bonus or a reward for their buying decision. This perception triggers positive emotions and reinforces the feeling of gratification associated with the purchase.

Many retailers utilize "free shipping thresholds" to encourage customers to spend more. For instance, a website may offer free shipping on orders over a certain dollar amount. Customers who are close to reaching this threshold often feel incentivized to add more items to their cart to unlock the free shipping reward. This approach not only increases the average order value for businesses but also leverages the psychology of reward-seeking in consumers.

Another psychological aspect of free shipping that makes

it appealing to consumers is the illusion of saving money. Shoppers tend to derive satisfaction from the idea that they are getting a better deal or saving money when they do not have to pay for shipping. Even if the product's price is slightly higher to cover the shipping cost, customers perceive it as a win.

This perception aligns with the principle of mental accounting, a concept in behavioral economics that suggests people mentally categorize their expenses and savings. When shipping is bundled into the product's price, customers mentally categorize the entire purchase as one cost, making it easier to see the savings in terms of shipping fees. As a result, free shipping gives customers a sense of financial prudence and encourages them to complete the purchase.

The psychology of free shipping also plays into the well-known phenomenon of FOMO, or the fear of missing out. When consumers see a limited-time offer for free shipping or a promotional code that promises this perk, they experience a heightened sense of urgency to take advantage of the deal. FOMO triggers the fear that they might lose out on a cost-saving opportunity, leading to impulsive buying decisions.

Retailers often leverage FOMO by incorporating countdown timers or displaying messages like "Limited Time Offer: Free Shipping Today!" on their websites. These tactics exploit the psychological need to be part of an exclusive group and the desire to avoid regret. As a result, free shipping not only influences purchasing decisions but also encourages customers to buy sooner rather than later.

In conclusion, the psychology of free shipping is a potent force in the world of e-commerce. It taps into various psychological principles, such as perceived value, the elimination of checkout hurdles, the sense of reward and gratification, the illusion of saving money, and the fear of missing out. Retailers recognize the power of free shipping in influencing consumer behavior, and they use it as a strategic tool to drive sales, increase average order values, and foster customer loyalty. As consumers, understanding the psychology behind free shipping can help us make more informed purchasing decisions and navigate the online shopping landscape with greater awareness.

The Ethical Consumer

There has been a significant shift in consumer preferences toward ethical and socially responsible products. Consumers are increasingly concerned about the environmental, social, and ethical impact of their purchasing decisions. Understanding the psychology of consumers who prioritize these products is crucial for businesses seeking to cater to this growing market segment. This section explores into the complexities of the psychology of ethical and socially responsible consumers, exploring the underlying motivations, values, and behaviors that drive their choices.

At the core of ethical and socially responsible consumer behavior are values and personal beliefs. These consumers are driven by a strong moral compass and a sense of responsibility toward society and the planet. They believe that their purchasing decisions can be a force for positive change, and their choices are guided by a desire to align their actions with their values.

Research in psychology has shown that individuals often make choices that reinforce their self-identity and values. Ethical consumers see their buying decisions as an extension of their moral principles. When they choose products that align with their values, they experience a sense of integrity and congruence.

Ethical and socially responsible consumers may prioritize values such as sustainability, environmental conservation, social justice, animal welfare, fair labor practices, and ethical sourcing. Their commitment to these values shapes their purchasing decisions and drives them to seek out products and brands that share their ethical concerns.

Another key psychological trait of ethical consumers is empathy and concern for others. They tend to be more empathetic toward those who are affected by the consequences of their consumption choices, whether it's factory workers, marginalized communities, or future generations. This empathy drives them to make choices that minimize harm and promote well-being.

Psychologically, empathy is associated with an individual's capacity to understand and share the feelings of others. Ethical consumers may envision the impact of their choices on the lives of those involved in the production and supply chain of a product. This emotional connection fuels their motivation to support ethical and socially responsible products.

Empathy also extends to concern for the environment and wildlife. Ethical consumers may feel a deep sense of responsibility for preserving the natural world and reducing their ecological footprint. This concern for the environment is a significant driver behind choices such as opting for eco-friendly packaging, reducing waste, and supporting sustainable agriculture practices.

Ethical and socially responsible consumers are often intrinsically motivated. They derive personal satisfaction and a sense of purpose from making ethical choices, even when external rewards or recognition are not present. This intrinsic motivation reflects their genuine commitment to their values.

Intrinsic motivation is associated with the fulfillment of psychological needs, such as autonomy, competence, and relatedness. Ethical consumers may perceive their choices as autonomous expressions of their values and beliefs, reinforcing their sense of self-determination.

Authenticity is a critical element in the psychology of these consumers. They are drawn to products and brands that authentically embody ethical and social responsibility principles. Authenticity builds trust and credibility, and consumers can discern when companies engage in "greenwashing" or insincere ethical marketing practices.

The psychology of ethical and socially responsible consumers is intertwined with their identity and social influence. These consumers often identify with a community of like-minded individuals who share similar values and concerns. Their ethical choices become part of their identity and a way to differentiate themselves from others.

Social influence plays a role in shaping ethical consumer behavior. When individuals observe peers or influencers making ethical choices, it can lead to a normative influence, where ethical behavior becomes the social norm. Social networks and online communities that champion ethical and sustainable living provide a platform for consumers to share information, tips, and recommendations.

The concept of identity-based motivation suggests that individuals are motivated to act in ways that are consistent with their self-identity. Ethical consumers view themselves as responsible global citizens, and their choices reinforce this identity. This identity reinforcement can lead to a sense of belonging to a community that shares their values.

Ethical and socially responsible consumers often go through a distinct decision-making process when selecting products. Their choices are influenced by various product attributes that align with their values and principles:

Transparency and Accountability: These consumers value transparency in product information, supply chains, and corporate practices. They prefer companies that are open about their ethical initiatives and are willing to be held accountable for their actions.

Sustainability: Sustainable product attributes, such as eco-friendly materials, renewable energy sources, and minimal environmental impact, are highly appealing to ethical consumers. They prioritize products that contribute to a more sustainable future.

Fair Trade and Ethical Sourcing: Ethical consumers look for fair trade certifications and ethical sourcing practices that ensure workers are paid fair wages and work in safe conditions. These attributes resonate with their values of social justice.

Animal Welfare: Concern for animal welfare drives choices such as cruelty-free, vegan, or ethically sourced animal products. Consumers may seek certifications like "cruelty-free" or "Animal Welfare Approved" when purchasing animal-related products.

Community Impact: Ethical consumers consider the impact of their choices on local and global communities. They support products and brands that give back to society through initiatives like community development, education, or charitable donations.

The psychology of consumers who prioritize ethical and socially responsible products is multifaceted and driven by a complex interplay of values, empathy, authenticity, identity, and product attributes. These consumers are motivated by a desire to make choices that align with their deeply held values and beliefs, as well as to contribute to a more just, sustainable, and compassionate world.

Understanding the psychology of ethical consumers is essential for businesses looking to engage with this growing market segment. To effectively connect with these consumers, companies must:

Authentically Align with Ethical Values: Demonstrate a sincere commitment to ethical and social responsibility principles in both product offerings and corporate practices.

Provide Transparency: Be transparent about product information, sourcing, and ethical initiatives, allowing consumers to make informed choices.

Foster Community and Identity: Create opportunities for consumers to connect with like-minded individuals who share their values, reinforcing a sense of identity and belonging.

Cultivate Empathy: Encourage empathy by sharing stories and narratives that highlight the positive impact of ethical and socially responsible choices.

Continuously Innovate: Stay attuned to evolving consumer values and preferences, and adapt product offerings and marketing strategies accordingly.

In conclusion, the psychology of consumers who prioritize ethical and socially responsible products reflects a fundamental shift in consumer behavior driven by values, empathy, authenticity, and a desire for positive social and environmental impact. Businesses that understand and respond to these psychological drivers can not only attract and retain conscious consumers but also contribute to a more sustainable and ethical global marketplace. Ethical and sustainable practices are not just a matter of meeting consumer demands; they are a path toward a more responsible and conscientious future for businesses and society as a whole.

Ethical Considerations in Marketing

C onsumer psychology and marketing play a pivotal role in shaping the decisions and behaviors of individuals in the marketplace. While these fields aim to understand consumer motivations and develop effective marketing strategies, they often grapple with ethical dilemmas. Ethical concerns in consumer psychology and marketing arise from the tension between business interests and consumer welfare. This section explores some of the most pressing ethical dilemmas in these fields, ranging from manipulative advertising to data privacy breaches. It also discusses the importance of ethical considerations in modern marketing practices.

One of the most prevalent ethical dilemmas in marketing is the use of manipulative advertising techniques to influence consumer behavior. These techniques may involve exploiting psychological vulnerabilities, such as fear, insecurity, or impulse buying tendencies, to persuade consumers to make purchases they might not otherwise make. For instance, ads that shame individuals for their appearance and then offer a product as a solution are ethically questionable.

Another form of manipulative advertising is the use of deceptive or false claims about a product's benefits or characteristics. Such practices mislead consumers and erode trust in the market. Ethical concerns also arise when marketing targets vulnerable populations, such as children, with advertising that exploits their limited understanding and decision-making capacity.

Addressing these ethical dilemmas requires a commitment to truthfulness, transparency, and consumer protection. Regulators and industry associations often play a crucial role in setting standards and guidelines to prevent manipulative advertising practices.

The collection and use of consumer data for marketing purposes have raised significant ethical concerns, especially in the era of digital marketing. Many companies collect vast amounts of personal information, including browsing habits, purchase history, and even location data, to create detailed consumer profiles. While data-driven marketing can improve personalization and relevance, it also poses risks to individuals' privacy.

Ethical dilemmas in data privacy include the unauthorized sharing or selling of consumer data to third parties, the lack of transparency about data collection practices, and the potential for data breaches. Consumers may be unaware of how their data is being used, leaving them vulnerable to manipulation or identity theft.

Ethical solutions to these dilemmas involve obtaining informed consent from consumers regarding data collection and usage, implementing robust data security measures, and adhering to data protection laws, such as the General Data Protection Regulation (GDPR) in Europe. Additionally, companies should prioritize the responsible handling of consumer data and communicate their privacy policies transparently.

Another ethical concern in consumer psychology and marketing involves the exploitation of consumer vulnerability. This can manifest in various ways, such as price gouging during crises, targeting individuals with addictive tendencies with products like gambling or alcohol, or taking advantage of cognitive biases like scarcity and social proof to drive sales.

Some online retailers may use dynamic pricing algorithms to adjust prices based on factors like location and browsing history, potentially charging higher prices to vulnerable or unsuspecting consumers. In such cases, the ethical dilemma lies in the imbalance of power and the potential for harm.

Ethical marketing practices require businesses to consider the impact of their strategies on vulnerable consumers and to avoid exploiting their weaknesses. Transparency in pricing, responsible advertising, and adherence to regulations that protect consumers from price discrimination are some measures that can address these concerns.

Ethical dilemmas in marketing extend beyond individual consumer interactions and also encompass broader societal and environmental considerations. Some businesses may engage in practices that prioritize short-term profits at the expense of long-term social and environmental well-being. Examples include promoting products that are harmful to health or the environment, greenwashing (misleading consumers about the sustainability of a product or company), or engaging in exploitative labor practices.

Ethical marketing requires businesses to align their strategies with principles of social responsibility and sustainability. This involves considering the environmental impact of products, ensuring fair labor practices throughout the supply chain, and providing accurate information about a product's ecological footprint. Ethical marketing also includes efforts to address social issues, such as promoting diversity and inclusion.

Ethical certification programs, sustainability reporting, and corporate social responsibility initiatives are tools that businesses can use to demonstrate their commitment to ethical and responsible practices.

Invasive marketing practices that interrupt consumers' daily lives or invade their personal spaces raise ethical concerns. These practices can include unsolicited telemarketing calls, spam emails, and aggressive pop-up advertisements that disrupt online experiences. Such intrusions can erode consumer autonomy and create negative perceptions of brands.

The use of psychological techniques, like nudging or persuasive design, to manipulate consumers into making decisions against their best interests is ethically problematic. For example, designing apps or websites to be intentionally addictive can lead to excessive use and harm to consumers' well-being.

Ethical marketing practices involve respecting consumer autonomy and preferences. This means offering opt-out mechanisms for marketing communications, providing clear and easy-to-find unsubscribe options, and avoiding deceptive or manipulative design elements in digital products.

Ethical dilemmas in consumer psychology and marketing arise from the tension between business interests and consumer welfare. Addressing these dilemmas requires a commitment to truthfulness, transparency, consumer protection, data privacy, social responsibility, and respecting consumer autonomy. In an era where consumers are increasingly informed and conscious of ethical issues, businesses that prioritize ethical marketing practices not only build trust but also contribute to a more responsible and sustainable marketplace. Ethical considerations should be an integral part of marketing strategies, guiding businesses toward practices that benefit both their bottom line and society as a whole.

Responsible marketing practices are integral to establishing and maintaining consumer trust in today's competitive and ethically conscious marketplace. Consumers are more informed and discerning than ever, and they expect businesses to not only deliver quality products and services but also to engage in ethical and transparent marketing. This section explores the relationship between responsible marketing practices and consumer trust. We will embark into the significance of ethical marketing, the impact of trust on consumer behavior, and specific strategies businesses can employ to build and nurture consumer trust through responsible marketing.

Responsible marketing involves adhering to ethical principles, transparency, and social responsibility in all aspects of a company's marketing efforts. It encompasses various practices, including truthful advertising, data privacy protection, sustainability, and fair treatment of consumers. Responsible marketing is not only a moral imperative but also a strategic one, as it directly influences consumer trust and brand reputation.

Businesses that engage in responsible marketing practices are more likely to build long-term relationships with consumers based on trust and loyalty. Such practices also contribute to positive brand perceptions and can enhance a company's competitive advantage. Conversely, unethical or deceptive marketing practices can lead to reputational damage, legal consequences, and loss of consumer trust, ultimately harming a company's bottom line.

Trust is a fundamental element of consumer decision-making. When consumers trust a brand, they are more likely to make purchases, remain loyal, and advocate for the brand. Trust in marketing manifests in several ways:

Product Trust: Consumers trust that a product will deliver the promised benefits and meet their expectations. Honest product representations and accurate claims are key to building and maintaining this trust.

Data Privacy Trust: In an age of data breaches and privacy concerns, consumers place great importance on trusting businesses with their personal information. Companies that prioritize data security and transparency in data collection and usage are more likely to gain consumers' trust.

Brand Trust: Brand trust extends beyond individual products and encompasses the overall reputation and ethical conduct of a brand. Consumers are more likely to support brands that align with their values and demonstrate social responsibility.

Marketing Trust: Trust in marketing itself is essential. When consumers perceive marketing communications as truthful and respectful, they are more likely to engage with and respond positively to those communications.

The impact of trust on consumer behavior cannot be overstated. It leads to higher customer retention rates, increased customer lifetime value, and positive word-of-mouth marketing—all of which contribute to a company's growth and success.

To build and nurture consumer trust through responsible marketing practices, businesses can employ a range of strategies:

Transparency: Transparency is a cornerstone of trust. Businesses should openly communicate their practices, values, and policies. This includes transparent pricing, clear product information, and honest advertising.

Data Privacy: Protecting consumer data is paramount. Companies should adhere to data protection regulations, obtain informed consent for data collection, and ensure data security. Communicating these efforts to consumers builds trust in data handling.

Sustainability and Social Responsibility: Demonstrating a commitment to sustainability and social responsibility resonates with consumers who prioritize ethical and environmentally conscious brands. Sharing initiatives, such as eco-friendly practices or support for charitable causes, can enhance trust.

Customer Engagement: Engaging with customers through open communication channels, responsive customer service, and personalized interactions fosters a sense of connection and trust. Actively listening to customer feedback and addressing concerns demonstrates commitment to customer satisfaction.

Ethical Advertising: Businesses should avoid deceptive advertising practices, exaggerated claims, or manipulative techniques. Honest and accurate advertising builds trust and credibility.

Authenticity: Authenticity in branding and marketing means being true to the company's values and identity. Authentic brands resonate with consumers who seek genuine and relatable experiences.

Consistency: Consistency in messaging and actions reinforces trust. Companies should align their marketing messages with their actual practices and consistently deliver on promises.

The digital age has introduced unique challenges and opportunities for responsible marketing. Online platforms, social media, and digital advertising have expanded the reach and impact of marketing efforts. However, they have also raised concerns about privacy, data security, and the proliferation of false information.

Digital Privacy: Clearly communicating data privacy policies and obtaining consent for data collection are essential in the digital space. Businesses must also safeguard consumer data from cyber threats.

Transparency in Online Advertising: Disclosing paid endorsements or sponsored content is vital to maintaining trust. Influencer marketing, in particular, requires transparency regarding compensated endorsements.

Combatting Misinformation: Businesses should avoid spreading false information or engaging in deceptive practices online. Ethical content creation and fact-checking contribute to a responsible online presence.

Online Customer Engagement: Engaging with customers through social media and digital platforms requires responsiveness and respectful communication. Companies should address customer inquiries and concerns promptly.

Online Reviews and Ratings: Encouraging authentic customer reviews and addressing negative feedback constructively can enhance trust online. Attempts to manipulate reviews harm trust and credibility.

Measuring and monitoring consumer trust is essential for businesses to assess the effectiveness of their responsible marketing efforts. Several key indicators can help evaluate trust levels:

Customer Satisfaction Surveys: Regular surveys can gauge overall customer satisfaction and trust in the brand. Questions about trust, reliability, and ethical practices should be included.

Net Promoter Score (NPS): NPS measures customer loyalty and the likelihood of recommending the brand to others. High NPS scores indicate a strong level of trust and satisfaction.

Online Reviews and Ratings: Monitoring online reviews and ratings can provide insights into consumer sentiments and trust levels. A high number of positive reviews indicates trust in the brand.

Customer Feedback and Complaints: Tracking customer feedback and addressing complaints effectively can improve trust. A decrease in the number of complaints suggests higher trust levels.

Repeat Purchases and Customer Retention: A high rate of repeat purchases and customer retention is a strong indicator of trust. Loyal customers trust the brand to consistently meet their needs.

Responsible marketing practices are indispensable for building and maintaining consumer trust in an increasingly ethical and transparent marketplace. Trust is not only a valuable asset but also a driving force behind consumer behavior and brand loyalty. Businesses that prioritize transparency, data privacy, sustainability, authenticity, and ethical advertising in their marketing efforts are more likely to earn the trust of their customers. In a world where consumers demand ethical conduct and responsible practices, responsible marketing is not only the right thing to do but also a strategic imperative for long-term success and brand resilience.

Online Shopping and E-commerce

T he advent of the internet has revolutionized the way consumers shop and interact with brands. Online shopping has become an integral part of modern life, and understanding the psychology behind online consumer behavior is crucial for businesses seeking to thrive in the digital landscape. This section explores the intricate factors that shape how consumers behave online, examining the psychological principles that drive decision-making, trust-building, and engagement. From the impact of user experience to the role of social influence, this discussion explores into the fascinating world of online consumer psychology.

Perhaps the most significant advantage of e-commerce is convenience. Shoppers can browse and make purchases from the comfort of their homes, avoiding the need to travel to physical stores. E-commerce platforms offer an extensive range of products from diverse brands and sellers. This vast selection caters to diverse consumer preferences and niches. Online shopping transcends geographical barriers, allowing consumers to access products and services from around the world. This accessibility is particularly valuable for consumers in remote or underserved areas. E-commerce platforms employ data analytics and AI algorithms to personalize the shopping experience. Tailored product recommendations and targeted marketing campaigns enhance user engagement.

User experience (UX) plays a pivotal role in shaping online consumer behavior. UX encompasses the overall experience a user has when interacting with a website, app, or online platform. A well-designed and user-friendly interface can significantly impact how consumers navigate and engage with a brand online.

The psychology behind UX is rooted in principles of cognitive psychology, which explore how individuals process information and make decisions. Websites that load quickly, provide intuitive navigation, and offer a visually pleasing layout can create a positive impression and reduce cognitive load for users. In contrast, websites with confusing layouts, slow loading times, or broken links may frustrate users, leading to high bounce rates and reduced conversions.

The use of psychological triggers, such as scarcity (limited-time offers) and social proof (customer reviews and testimonials), can enhance the user experience and encourage consumer behavior like making a purchase or subscribing to a newsletter.

Building trust online is a critical aspect of consumer behavior. Consumers often face uncertainty and skepticism when transacting with unfamiliar online businesses or sharing personal information. To overcome these barriers, websites must establish credibility and foster trust.

The psychology of trust online is closely tied to factors such as website design, security measures, and the clarity of communication. For instance, a website that displays trust seals, like SSL certificates, can signal to consumers that their data will be protected, reducing anxiety related to security. Transparent and easily accessible contact information, including physical addresses and customer service numbers, also contributes to trust, as it demonstrates a commitment to open communication.

Online reviews and ratings from other consumers can significantly influence trust and purchasing decisions. Positive reviews and high ratings serve as social proof, assuring potential customers of a brand's reliability and quality. Conversely, negative reviews or a lack of reviews can deter consumers, raising doubts about the brand's authenticity.

Personalization is a powerful psychological tool that shapes online consumer behavior. The idea behind personalization is to tailor content, recommendations, and offers to the individual preferences and behaviors of each user. This approach leverages principles of cognitive psychology related to attention, memory, and motivation.

Personalization enhances user engagement by presenting content that is relevant and interesting to the individual. For example, an e-commerce website may recommend products based on a user's browsing history or purchase history. This not only streamlines the shopping process but also makes the user feel understood and valued, increasing the likelihood of conversions.

Behavioral targeting is a closely related concept that uses data on a user's online behavior, such as the websites they visit and the products they view, to deliver targeted advertisements. These ads are more likely to capture a user's attention and prompt action because they align with the user's demonstrated interests.

The use of personalization and behavioral targeting also raises ethical concerns about privacy and data security, highlighting the importance of transparent data usage and user consent.

Social influence plays a significant role in online consumer behavior. The concept of social proof, popularized by psychologist Robert Cialdini, highlights the tendency of individuals to conform to the behaviors and preferences of others. Online, this phenomenon manifests in various ways.

User-generated content, such as reviews, ratings, and testimonials, serves as a form of social proof that can influence purchasing decisions. Positive reviews and endorsements from peers or influencers can sway consumer behavior by reinforcing the perceived value and quality of a product or service.

Fear of Missing Out (FOMO) is another psychological trigger

often leveraged in online marketing. FOMO capitalizes on the fear that one might miss out on something desirable or beneficial. Limited-time offers, countdown timers, and messages like "only a few left in stock" create a sense of urgency, compelling users to take immediate action to avoid missing out on a perceived opportunity.

Social media also plays a significant role in shaping online consumer behavior. Consumers are influenced by the content and recommendations of friends, family, and influencers they follow. Social media platforms have become integral channels for product discovery, with users often seeking inspiration and validation from their social networks.

Online consumer behavior is often influenced by various cognitive shortcuts or decision-making heuristics that people employ to simplify choices. Two prominent heuristics are price-based decision-making and brand loyalty.

Price-based decision-making involves consumers seeking the best deal or the lowest price when shopping online. E-commerce platforms often capitalize on this heuristic by prominently displaying prices, discounts, and special offers. Price comparison websites and apps further facilitate this heuristic by allowing users to easily compare prices across multiple retailers.

Brand loyalty is another influential heuristic that impacts online consumer behavior. Consumers tend to stick with familiar brands, as they perceive them as reliable and trustworthy. Successful online businesses invest in building and maintaining their brand identity to foster loyalty and encourage repeat purchases. Brand recognition and reputation can be powerful drivers of consumer behavior, even in the digital realm.

Understanding the psychology of online consumer behavior is essential for businesses seeking to thrive in the digital age. User experience, trust-building, personalization, social influence, and decision-making heuristics are among the key factors that shape how consumers behave online. By applying these psychological principles, businesses can optimize their online presence, create engaging user experiences, and effectively influence consumer decisions, ultimately leading to increased conversions and long-term customer loyalty. In a rapidly evolving digital landscape, staying attuned to the psychology of online consumer behavior is a vital component of success for businesses of all sizes and industries.

In the increasingly competitive world of online retail, having a well-optimized e-commerce website is essential for attracting and retaining customers. Optimization encompasses a wide range of strategies and techniques aimed at enhancing the overall user experience, improving website performance, and driving higher conversion rates. This section explores five key strategies for optimizing e-commerce websites, from improving site speed and mobile responsiveness to enhancing product listings and implementing effective SEO practices. By applying these strategies, businesses can create a seamless shopping experience that maximizes revenue and customer satisfaction.

Website speed is a critical factor in e-commerce optimization. Slow-loading pages can lead to high bounce rates, increased cart abandonment, and a negative impact on search engine rankings. To optimize website speed and performance, businesses should consider the following strategies:

Content Delivery Network (CDN): Implementing a CDN can distribute website content to servers in different geographical locations, reducing server response times and speeding up page loading.

Compressed Images: Compressing images can significantly reduce their file size without sacrificing quality, resulting in faster load times.

Minimization of HTTP Requests: Reducing the number of HTTP requests by minimizing the use of external scripts and stylesheets can improve page load speed.

Caching: Implementing browser and server-side caching can store frequently accessed data, reducing the need to reload it with each visit.

Optimized Code: Streamlining website code and minimizing unnecessary scripts can help reduce load times.

Regular Performance Testing: Conducting regular performance tests using tools like Google PageSpeed Insights or GTmetrix can identify areas for improvement.

With the increasing prevalence of mobile shopping, having a mobile-responsive e-commerce website is no longer optional. Mobile optimization is essential for providing a seamless and user-friendly experience to mobile shoppers. Key strategies for mobile optimization include:

Responsive Design: Implementing a responsive design ensures that the website adapts to various screen sizes and orientations, providing a consistent user experience across devices.

Mobile-Friendly Navigation: Simplify navigation and minimize the need for excessive scrolling on mobile devices to enhance usability.

Optimized Images and Media: Ensure that images and media are appropriately sized and compressed for mobile screens to reduce load times.

Mobile Checkout Optimization: Streamline the checkout process for mobile users, minimizing the number of steps and input fields required to complete a purchase.

Mobile-First Indexing: Prioritize mobile optimization for better search engine rankings, as search engines increasingly use mobile-first indexing.

Product listings are at the heart of e-commerce websites, and optimizing them can significantly impact sales. Strategies for effective product listings include:

High-Quality Images: Use high-resolution images that showcase products from different angles and include zoom functionality.

Detailed Descriptions: Provide comprehensive product descriptions that highlight key features, benefits, and specifications, helping customers make informed decisions.

User Reviews and Ratings: Incorporate user-generated reviews and ratings to build trust and provide social proof of product quality.

Clear Pricing and Promotions: Display pricing clearly and prominently, and highlight any special promotions or discounts.

Related Products and Cross-Selling: Suggest related products or accessories to encourage upselling and cross-selling.

Product Availability: Clearly indicate whether products are in stock or provide estimated delivery times to manage customer expectations.

SEO is a critical component of e-commerce optimization, as it helps improve organic search rankings and drives organic traffic to the website. Effective SEO strategies include:

Keyword Research: Conduct thorough keyword research to identify relevant keywords and phrases that potential customers are likely to use when searching for products.

On-Page Optimization: Optimize product pages, category pages, and other content with relevant keywords, meta titles, meta descriptions, and header tags.

High-Quality Content: Create informative and engaging content, such as blog posts, buying guides, and product descriptions, to enhance the website's authority and relevance.

Mobile Optimization: Ensure that the website is mobile-friendly, as mobile optimization is a significant factor in search engine rankings.

Link Building: Build high-quality backlinks from reputable websites to improve the website's authority and credibility.

Site Structure: Create a logical and user-friendly site structure with clear navigation and well-organized product categories.

Conversion rate optimization focuses on maximizing the percentage of website visitors who complete desired actions, such as making a purchase, signing up for a newsletter, or requesting more information. Effective CRO strategies include:

A/B Testing: Conduct A/B tests to compare different versions of web pages, product pages, and checkout processes to identify the most effective elements.

Optimized Call-to-Actions (CTAs): Use clear and persuasive CTAs that guide users toward desired actions, such as "Add to Cart" or "Buy Now."

Checkout Process Simplification: Streamline the checkout process by reducing the number of steps and minimizing required form fields.

Trust Signals: Display trust signals, such as secure payment icons, SSL certificates, and return policies, to build trust with customers.

Cart Abandonment Strategies: Implement cart abandonment emails and incentives to encourage users to complete their purchases.

Personalization: Use data-driven insights to personalize recommendations, offers, and content based on user behavior and preferences.

Optimizing e-commerce websites is a multifaceted endeavor that encompasses various strategies aimed at enhancing user experience, improving website performance, and increasing conversion rates. Website speed and performance, mobile responsiveness, effective product listings, SEO, and CRO are all integral components of a successful e-commerce optimization strategy. By implementing these strategies, businesses can create a competitive advantage, attract and retain customers, and drive higher revenue in the highly competitive world of online retail. In an ever-evolving digital landscape, continuous optimization is key to staying ahead and meeting the evolving needs of online shoppers.

How technology influences consumer behavior

Technology has become an omnipresent force in our lives, significantly influencing the way we make decisions and interact with products, services, and brands. As we navigate an increasingly digitized world, the impact of technology on consumer behavior is profound and multi-faceted. This section explores how technology, spanning from e-commerce platforms to social media and artificial intelligence, shapes and transforms consumer behavior. We will explore into five key areas where technology exerts its influence: information access, shopping habits, decision-making processes, brand engagement, and privacy concerns.

One of the most evident ways technology influences consumer behavior is through the democratization of information access. In the pre-digital era, consumers relied on limited sources for product information, primarily through traditional advertising and word-of-mouth. Today, a wealth of information is at our fingertips, thanks to search engines, online reviews, and social media platforms.

Consumers can now research products, read reviews, and compare prices effortlessly, giving them more power and control over their purchasing decisions. The rise of user-generated content on platforms like Yelp and Amazon Reviews has amplified the impact of word-of-mouth, making peer recommendations a vital part of the consumer journey. This easy access to information has created a more informed and discerning consumer base, forcing businesses to prioritize transparency and quality.

The proliferation of e-commerce has radically transformed shopping habits. Online retailers offer convenience, accessibility, and a vast array of choices, challenging traditional brick-and-mortar stores. Technology has made it possible for consumers to shop at any time, from anywhere, and on various devices, eliminating geographical barriers and expanding the reach of businesses.

Moreover, the concept of the omnichannel experience has blurred the lines between online and offline shopping. Consumers now expect a seamless journey, seamlessly transitioning from researching products online to experiencing them in-store or vice versa. This shift in shopping habits has prompted retailers to invest in creating a consistent brand experience across all touchpoints and enhancing their digital presence to remain competitive.

Technology has not only changed where and how consumers shop but also how they make decisions. Personalization, driven by data analytics and artificial intelligence, has become a central element in the consumer experience. Algorithms analyze vast amounts of data, including past behavior, preferences, and online activity, to tailor product recommendations and marketing messages to individual consumers.

This personalization has the potential to streamline the decision-making process by presenting consumers with options that are highly relevant to their interests and needs. At the same time, it raises concerns about privacy and the potential for filter bubbles, where consumers are only exposed to information that aligns with their existing beliefs and preferences.

Social media has emerged as a powerful platform for brand engagement and consumer influence. Platforms like Facebook, Instagram, and TikTok have transformed the way consumers discover, interact with, and endorse products and services. Influencer marketing, in particular, has gained prominence, as individuals with substantial followings leverage their online presence to endorse products and shape consumer preferences.

Consumers not only passively receive marketing messages but also actively participate in brand conversations. User-generated content, hashtags, and challenges encourage consumers to engage with brands and become advocates. This dynamic shift in brand-consumer interactions places greater importance on authenticity and transparency, as consumers are quick to spot inauthentic or disingenuous efforts by brands.

While technology offers numerous benefits to consumers, it also raises critical privacy concerns and ethical considerations. The collection, storage, and use of personal data have come under intense scrutiny, leading to debates about data privacy and security. Consumers are increasingly concerned about how their information is used, leading to the implementation of data protection regulations like GDPR and CCPA.

Privacy breaches, data leaks, and the misuse of personal information erode consumer trust and can have lasting consequences for brands. Consumers are becoming more vigilant about sharing their data and are gravitating toward businesses that prioritize data security and transparent data practices. Balancing the benefits of data-driven personalization with the ethical responsibility to protect consumer data is a complex challenge faced by businesses and policymakers alike.

Technology's influence on consumer behavior is undeniable, reshaping how consumers access information, make purchasing decisions, engage with brands, and grapple with privacy concerns. As technology continues to evolve, so too will its impact on consumer behavior, presenting both opportunities and challenges for businesses. To thrive in this digital landscape, companies must adapt to changing consumer expectations, prioritize transparency and data security, and navigate the delicate balance between personalization and privacy. Understanding and harnessing the transformative power of technology is essential for businesses seeking to remain competitive and relevant in the ever-changing world of consumer behavior.

Influence of Social Media
on Consumer Behavior

The emergence and widespread adoption of social media platforms have transformed the landscape of consumer behavior. Social media has become an integral part of our daily lives, offering not only social interaction but also a powerful medium for businesses to engage with consumers. This section explores the multifaceted influence of social media on consumer behavior, dissecting the key factors, mechanisms, and implications that shape the digital marketplace. By understanding these dynamics, we gain insight into the profound impact of social media on how consumers make choices and interact with brands.

The prevalence of social media is undeniable, with billions of users worldwide actively engaging on platforms such as Facebook, Instagram, Twitter, and TikTok. This ubiquity has given rise to new opportunities and challenges for businesses and consumers alike.

Social media platforms enable individuals to connect, communicate, and share content with a global audience. This connectivity has created virtual communities based on shared interests and affiliations.

Information Dissemination: Social media serves as a rapid and far-reaching information dissemination tool. News, trends, and content can go viral within seconds, influencing public opinion and consumer choices.

User-Generated Content: Consumers are no longer passive recipients of information; they actively create and share content. User-generated content, including product reviews and testimonials, wields significant influence.

Business Presence: Companies recognize the importance of a social media presence. Businesses use these platforms for marketing, customer engagement, and market research.

Several factors contribute to the influential power of social media on consumer behavior:

Social Proof: The concept of social proof suggests that people tend to conform to the actions and opinions of others. When consumers see their peers endorsing or using a product on social media, it creates a sense of trust and legitimacy.

Influencer Marketing: Social media influencers, individuals with a substantial following and niche expertise, play a pivotal role in shaping consumer behavior. They can sway opinions, promote products, and drive engagement.

Targeted Advertising: Social media platforms employ advanced algorithms to track user behavior and preferences. This data is used to deliver highly targeted advertisements, increasing the likelihood of conversions.

FOMO (Fear of Missing Out): Social media often showcases curated and idealized versions of people's lives. This creates a sense of FOMO, prompting consumers to make purchases or participate in trends to feel included.

Consumer Engagement: The two-way communication facilitated by social media allows businesses to engage directly with consumers. Responding to inquiries, addressing concerns, and fostering a sense of community can influence buying decisions.

The consumer journey has undergone a significant transformation due to social media's influence. It now involves multiple touchpoints and interactions across various platforms.

Discovery: Consumers often discover new products or services through social media feeds, sponsored content, or recommendations from friends and influencers.

Research: Social media provides a platform for consumers to conduct research by reading reviews, comparing prices, and seeking opinions from their network.

Engagement: Consumers may engage with a brand through comments, likes, or direct messages, creating a sense of familiarity and connection.

Purchase: Many social media platforms now offer seamless shopping experiences, allowing consumers to make purchases without leaving the platform.

Post-Purchase: After a purchase, consumers may share their experiences on social media, providing valuable feedback and influencing others.

While social media's influence on consumer behavior offers numerous benefits, it also presents challenges and ethical considerations:

Privacy Concerns: The collection and use of personal data for targeted advertising raise privacy concerns. Consumers worry about their data being exploited without their consent.

Misinformation and Fake News: Social media can facilitate the rapid spread of misinformation and fake news, leading to misguided consumer choices and societal harm.

Addictive Behavior: The addictive nature of social media, driven by algorithms designed to maximize engagement, can lead to excessive screen time and impulsive buying decisions.

Mental Health Impact: Excessive use of social media has been linked to mental health issues, such as anxiety and depression, which can influence consumer behavior and well-being.

Filter Bubbles: Social media algorithms often create filter bubbles, where users are exposed to content that aligns with their existing beliefs and preferences, limiting exposure to diverse perspectives.

As social media continues to evolve, several future trends and implications emerge:

E-commerce Integration: Social commerce is expected to grow, with platforms offering more seamless shopping experiences, including in-app purchases and checkout.

Virtual Reality (VR) and Augmented Reality (AR): VR and AR technologies will enhance immersive shopping experiences, allowing consumers to "try before they buy" virtually.

Regulatory Oversight: Governments and regulatory bodies are likely to implement stricter regulations on data privacy and content moderation on social media platforms.

Sustainability: Consumers' growing awareness of environmental issues is expected to influence brand choices, with sustainable and socially responsible brands gaining prominence.

Rise of Niche Communities: Niche online communities and micro-influencers will gain influence, allowing for hyper-targeted marketing and consumer engagement.

The influence of social media on consumer behavior is undeniable and continues to shape the digital marketplace in profound ways. Its ubiquity, coupled with factors like social proof, influencer marketing, and targeted advertising, has reshaped how consumers discover, research, engage with, and make purchases from brands. While the impact is largely positive, there are challenges related to privacy, misinformation, and mental health that need to be addressed. As social media evolves and new technologies emerge, the consumer landscape will continue to change, making it imperative for businesses, regulators, and consumers themselves to adapt and navigate this ever-evolving digital terrain. Understanding the dynamics of social media's influence on consumer behavior is key to thriving in this dynamic and interconnected world.

The Psychology of Word-of-Mouth

Word-of-mouth (WOM) has been a potent force in shaping human behavior and decisions for centuries. Whether it's a glowing recommendation from a friend about a new restaurant or a cautionary tale from a colleague about a bad experience with a product, the impact of personal recommendations cannot be overstated. In the realm of psychology, understanding the intricate workings of word-of-mouth has been a subject of keen interest. This phenomenon touches upon various aspects of human psychology, including trust, social influence, cognitive biases, and persuasion. In this exploration, we examine the psychology of word-of-mouth, uncovering the underlying mechanisms that make it such a powerful force in shaping our choices and behaviors.

At the heart of word-of-mouth lies the concept of trust. When we receive a recommendation from someone we know and trust, it carries a significant weight in our decision-making process. This trust is often rooted in the psychology of social proof, a phenomenon first popularized by psychologist Robert Cialdini. Social proof suggests that people tend to follow the actions and behaviors of others, especially in uncertain or unfamiliar situations. When a friend or family member speaks highly of a product or service, their endorsement provides a sense of assurance and reduces the perceived risk associated with trying something new.

Psychologically, this trust can be explained by the concept of the "mere exposure effect." This phenomenon posits that the more we are exposed to something, the more we tend to like it and trust it. In the context of word-of-mouth, the repeated positive mentions of a particular brand or product by those we trust reinforce our perception of its value and reliability. In essence, word-of-mouth acts as a conduit for the transfer of trust, making it a powerful tool for marketers and a crucial factor in consumer decision-making.

Word-of-mouth isn't just about trust; it's also deeply entwined with cognitive biases that influence how we perceive and process information. One of the most prevalent biases at play in word-of-mouth is confirmation bias. This bias leads us to seek out information that confirms our existing beliefs and attitudes while disregarding or downplaying information that contradicts them. When a friend or acquaintance recommends a product or service that aligns with our preconceived notions, it reinforces our confirmation bias and strengthens our resolve to follow their advice.

The availability heuristic plays a significant role in word-of-mouth recommendations. This cognitive bias leads us to rely on readily available information when making decisions, often favoring information that comes from personal anecdotes and stories. When someone shares a memorable and positive experience with a particular brand or product, it becomes more accessible in our minds, swaying our decisions in its favor. This phenomenon highlights the persuasive power of vivid and emotionally resonant word-of-mouth narratives.

Word-of-mouth is not solely a rational process; it also operates on a deep emotional level. Humans are inherently social creatures, wired to connect with others and empathize with their experiences. When we hear a friend's heartfelt recommendation or listen to their personal story about how a product or service positively impacted their life, we tap into our capacity for empathy. This emotional resonance creates a powerful bond between the storyteller and the listener.

In the field of psychology, this emotional aspect of word-of-mouth can be linked to mirror neurons, which fire both when we perform an action and when we observe someone else perform that same action. In the context of word-of-mouth, when we hear about a positive experience, our mirror neurons may activate, allowing us to vicariously experience the pleasure and satisfaction described by the storyteller. This emotional connection not only enhances the impact of word-of-mouth but also fosters a sense of camaraderie and trust within social networks.

Word-of-mouth isn't just about sharing personal experiences; it also involves persuasion and information processing. When individuals share recommendations, they often employ persuasive techniques to influence the opinions and actions of others. These techniques may include storytelling, using vivid language, and appealing to emotions.

The psychology of persuasion, as outlined by Robert Cialdini in his book "Influence," highlights several principles at work in word-of-mouth persuasion. For instance, the principle of reciprocity suggests that when someone does something for us, we feel obligated to return the favor. In the context of word-of-mouth, if a friend goes out of their way to recommend a product or service, we may feel compelled to reciprocate by trying it out. Similarly, the principle of scarcity suggests that people are more attracted to things that are perceived as rare or in limited supply. If a friend suggests that a product is in high demand or available for a limited time, it can increase our desire to obtain it.

In the digital age, word-of-mouth has taken on new dimensions through the phenomenon of virality. Social media platforms and online communities have amplified the speed and reach of word-of-mouth recommendations. The psychology behind virality often involves a combination of factors, including novelty, emotion, and social sharing.

Novelty is a fundamental driver of virality. When people come across something new, unique, or unexpected, they are more likely to share it with their networks. Additionally, content that evokes strong emotions, whether positive (e.g., joy, awe) or negative (e.g., anger, outrage), tends to be shared more extensively. Emotionally charged content captures people's attention and prompts them to pass it along to others who may experience similar emotions.

Social networks play a pivotal role in the spread of word-of-mouth in the digital realm. The "small world phenomenon" suggests that we are all interconnected through a relatively small number of social ties. When someone shares a recommendation or content within their network, it can quickly cascade through these connections, reaching a wide audience in a short time. This interconnectedness amplifies the influence of word-of-mouth, turning it into a powerful force that can shape public opinion and drive consumer behavior on a massive scale.

The psychology of word-of-mouth is a multifaceted and dynamic field that draws from various aspects of human behavior, cognition, and emotion. Trust and social proof underscore the importance of personal recommendations in decision-making, while cognitive biases like confirmation bias and the availability heuristic shape how we process and respond to word-of-mouth information. The emotional impact and empathy involved in storytelling deepen the connection between storytellers and listeners, while persuasive techniques influence our actions and choices.

Word-of-mouth has evolved into a viral force, spreading through social networks and reshaping the way we discover and engage with products, services, and ideas. As individuals continue to navigate a world inundated with information and choices, understanding the psychology of word-of-mouth becomes increasingly vital for marketers, businesses, and anyone seeking to influence or be influenced by the power of personal recommendations. By harnessing the principles and mechanisms that underlie word-of-mouth, we can better appreciate its role in our lives and make more informed decisions in an interconnected and information-rich world.

Cross-Generational Consumer Behavior

Consumer decisions play a pivotal role in shaping economies and industries, and they are profoundly influenced by the unique characteristics and experiences of different generations. Each generation, from the Silent Generation to Generation Z, has distinct values, preferences, and attitudes that drive their purchasing behaviors. In this section, we will delve into how different generations approach consumer decisions, exploring the factors that shape their choices, and how they adapt to evolving market dynamics. By examining these generational perspectives, we can gain valuable insights into consumer behavior, which can be invaluable for businesses and marketers striving to connect with diverse consumer groups.

The Silent Generation (1928-1945), born during the tumultuous years of the Great Depression and World War II, developed distinct consumer habits characterized by frugality, loyalty, and a focus on necessity. Growing up during times of economic hardship, they learned to value thriftiness and were often cautious spenders. Their loyalty to brands and products is deeply rooted in the belief that quality and durability are essential. This generation, now in their late 70s to 90s, still values face-to-face interactions and tends to rely on traditional media for information.

When making consumer decisions, the Silent Generation often looks for well-established brands and places a premium on the reliability and durability of products. They prefer in-person shopping experiences and are less influenced by digital marketing and online reviews. For businesses targeting this generation, emphasizing quality, longevity, and personalized customer service can be particularly effective.

Baby Boomers (1946-1964), the post-World War II generation, have seen significant shifts in consumer culture throughout their lives. They grew up in a time of economic growth and witnessed the rise of television advertising and mass consumerism. This experience has made them pragmatic consumers who prioritize value for their money. Baby Boomers are also known for their loyalty to brands but are more open to trying new products and services compared to the Silent Generation.

Baby Boomers approach consumer decisions with a balanced perspective, considering both traditional and digital sources of information. They value recommendations from friends and family but also rely on online reviews and social media to gather information. To connect with Baby Boomers, businesses should highlight the value and reliability of their offerings while maintaining a strong online presence.

Generation X (1965-1980), often referred to as the "latchkey generation," came of age during a period of social and technological change. They are known for their independence, skepticism, and adaptability. Growing up with the emergence of cable television, video games, and the personal computer, they are comfortable with technology but not as digitally immersed as younger generations.

When making consumer decisions, Generation X tends to be more practical and focused on efficiency. They value convenience and often look for products and services that can simplify their busy lives. While they still consider traditional advertising and word-of-mouth recommendations, they are more likely to conduct online research and read product reviews before making a purchase. To reach Generation X, businesses should emphasize convenience, efficiency, and the quality of their products or services.

Millennials (1981-1996), often referred to as the "digital natives," have grown up in the era of the internet, smartphones, and social media. They are characterized by their tech-savviness, environmental consciousness, and a preference for experiences over material possessions. Millennials tend to be more socially conscious consumers and are willing to support brands that align with their values.

When making consumer decisions, Millennials are heavily influenced by online content, social media, and peer recommendations. They value authenticity and are quick to dismiss traditional advertising that feels insincere or overly promotional. To connect with Millennials, businesses should prioritize social responsibility, engage in transparent and authentic marketing, and maintain a strong online presence across various platforms.

Generation Z (1997-present), the youngest consumer group, is entering adulthood with a unique set of characteristics shaped by technology and globalization. They are true digital natives, having grown up with smartphones, social media, and instant access to information. Gen Z is known for its diversity, entrepreneurial spirit, and desire for personalization.

When making consumer decisions, Generation Z relies heavily on online sources, social media influencers, and peer recommendations. They prioritize individuality and are more likely to support brands that offer personalized experiences and products. For businesses targeting Gen Z, it's crucial to embrace digital marketing strategies, emphasize authenticity, and demonstrate a commitment to social and environmental causes.

Generational differences in consumer decision-making stem from a combination of historical events, technological advancements, and cultural shifts. Understanding these differences is essential for businesses and marketers aiming to connect with diverse consumer groups. While each generation has its unique preferences and values, successful businesses will adapt their strategies to effectively engage with multiple generations simultaneously. By recognizing and respecting these generational perspectives, companies can build stronger brand connections and foster customer loyalty across the spectrum of age groups in the market.

Consumer Behavior in a Global Context

C onsumer choices are not solely determined by individual preferences or economic factors. Culture and international factors play a pivotal role in shaping the decisions consumers make when selecting products and services. Culture encompasses a society's values, beliefs, customs, and traditions, while international factors encompass global economic, political, and social forces. In this section, we will explore how these two intertwined elements impact consumer choices, from product preferences to purchasing behaviors, and how businesses can navigate this complex landscape to better cater to diverse markets.

Culture is a profound influencer of consumer behavior, as it shapes individuals' perceptions, attitudes, and values. Cultural factors that impact consumer choices include:

Cultural Values: Different cultures place varying degrees of importance on values such as individualism, collectivism, time orientation, and materialism. For example, in collectivist cultures, family and community needs often take precedence over individual desires, affecting product choices.

Social Norms and Customs: Cultural norms dictate what is considered acceptable or taboo behavior within a society. These norms influence consumer choices by guiding individuals towards products and services that align with their culture's expectations.

Religious Beliefs: Religion can significantly impact consumer choices. For example, dietary restrictions associated with certain religions affect food and beverage preferences, leading to the popularity of kosher, halal, or vegetarian products.

Language and Communication: Language is an essential cultural element that influences advertising and marketing. Adapting marketing materials to the local language and communication style is crucial for reaching diverse audiences effectively.

Symbols and Rituals: Cultural symbols and rituals often carry deep meaning. Brands that incorporate these symbols and rituals into their products or marketing campaigns can resonate more strongly with consumers from specific cultural backgrounds.

Consumer choices are increasingly influenced by international factors due to globalization and interconnected economies. Key international factors that impact consumer choices include:

Economic Conditions: Economic stability, income levels, and currency exchange rates directly affect consumers' purchasing power and, consequently, their choices. Economic downturns may lead to reduced spending and altered preferences for more affordable products.

Political Climate: Political instability, trade agreements, and government policies can disrupt supply chains, affecting product availability and prices. Consumers may adapt their choices based on the political climate of their region.

Global Trends and Fads: Rapid communication and the spread of trends through social media have led to the globalization of fashion, entertainment, and lifestyle choices. Consumers worldwide are increasingly influenced by global trends, leading to the homogenization of certain product preferences.

Cultural Exchange: Increased cultural exchange between nations has led to a greater appreciation for international cuisines, fashion, and entertainment. This exposure often leads to consumers seeking out products and experiences from other cultures.

Environmental Concerns: International awareness of environmental issues has spurred a global movement towards sustainable and eco-friendly consumer choices. Consumers worldwide are increasingly choosing products that align with these values.

Businesses seeking to thrive in diverse global markets must consider cultural and international factors in their marketing and business strategies. Some strategies include:

Cultural Sensitivity: Understanding the cultural nuances of a target market is essential. Businesses should adapt their messaging, branding, and product offerings to resonate with local cultures.

Localization: Tailoring products and services to meet the specific needs and preferences of a local market can significantly boost consumer acceptance and loyalty.

Global Branding: Some brands successfully use global branding that transcends cultural boundaries. These brands often focus on universal themes like happiness, family, or adventure.

Market Research: Conducting thorough market research to understand cultural and international factors is crucial. This includes consumer preferences, market trends, and cultural sensitivities.

Ethical Considerations: Businesses should also be mindful of ethical concerns that may arise in international markets. Ethical practices can enhance brand reputation and consumer trust.

Several companies have excelled in navigating the complex interplay of culture and international factors. For instance:

McDonald's: McDonald's tailors its menu to local tastes in various countries, offering items like the McSpaghetti in the Philippines and the McAloo Tikki burger in India. This localization strategy enables the brand to connect with consumers on a cultural level.

Coca-Cola: Coca-Cola is a global brand that successfully embraces cultural diversity while maintaining a consistent global identity. Their "Share a Coke" campaign featured personalized labels with common names in various languages, encouraging consumers to connect through the brand.

IKEA: IKEA adapts its furniture designs to suit the preferences and needs of consumers in different countries. For instance, they produce smaller, space-saving furniture for markets where living spaces are limited.

Nike: Nike's marketing campaigns often celebrate the cultural diversity and individuality of athletes worldwide. This approach resonates with consumers from various cultural backgrounds.

Culture and international factors wield immense influence over consumer choices, shaping preferences, values, and behaviors. Businesses that recognize and adapt to these factors stand to gain a competitive advantage in the global marketplace. By understanding the cultural nuances and international dynamics of their target markets, companies can develop effective marketing strategies, tailor their products and services, and build meaningful connections with consumers from diverse backgrounds. In a world marked by globalization and cultural diversity, the ability to navigate and embrace these influences is key to success in the consumer-driven marketplace.

Consumer Behavior in
Services and Experiences

In a competitive business landscape, providing excellent products and services is no longer enough to differentiate a brand. To stand out and build lasting customer loyalty, companies must focus on creating memorable service experiences. A memorable service experience goes beyond meeting expectations; it leaves a lasting impression that customers cherish and share with others. In this section, we will explore five key strategies that businesses can employ to craft exceptional service experiences that captivate customers and foster long-term relationships.

One of the most effective strategies for creating memorable service experiences is personalization. Recognizing that each customer is unique and tailoring services accordingly can make a significant difference. Here are some ways to infuse personalization into service delivery:

Customer Data Analysis: Utilize customer data and analytics to understand individual preferences, purchase history, and behavior. This information can help in customizing recommendations and offerings.

Personalized Communication: Address customers by their names, send personalized emails or messages, and acknowledge special occasions like birthdays or anniversaries.

Customized Solutions: Offer personalized product recommendations or service options based on the customer's needs and preferences.

Feedback and Listening: Actively seek and listen to customer feedback. Use their insights to make improvements and demonstrate that their opinions matter.

Empower Frontline Staff: Equip employees with the authority and resources to make on-the-spot decisions to accommodate unique customer requests or resolve issues swiftly.

Behind every memorable service experience are well-trained and empowered employees who genuinely care about customer satisfaction. Businesses should invest in training programs that emphasize the importance of empathy, active listening, and problem-solving skills. Empowered employees are more likely to go the extra mile to create positive memories for customers. Key elements of employee training and empowerment include:

Emphasize Soft Skills: Training should focus on developing soft skills like empathy, effective communication, and conflict resolution, which are essential for handling diverse customer interactions.

Customer-Centric Culture: Create a company culture that values and rewards exceptional customer service. Recognize and celebrate employees who consistently deliver memorable experiences.

Continuous Learning: Provide ongoing training and development opportunities to keep employees updated on the latest industry trends and customer service techniques.

Empowerment: Encourage employees to make judgment calls and resolve issues without requiring managerial approval in every instance. This autonomy can lead to quicker problem resolution and enhanced customer satisfaction.

Feedback Loops: Establish feedback mechanisms for employees to share insights and suggestions for improving service delivery.

Consistency is key to creating memorable service experiences. Customers should receive a consistently high level of service every time they interact with a brand, regardless of the channel or location. Achieving consistency requires:

Standardized Processes: Develop standardized service processes and guidelines to ensure uniformity in service delivery across all touchpoints.

Training and Onboarding: Train all employees, including new hires, on the company's service standards and expectations to maintain a consistent service culture.

Technology Integration: Use technology solutions, such as customer relationship management (CRM) systems, to track customer interactions and ensure continuity in communication and service provision.

Feedback and Quality Assurance: Implement quality control measures and regularly monitor service interactions through customer feedback and performance evaluations.

Flexibility Within Frameworks: While maintaining consistency, allow employees the flexibility to adapt service delivery to individual customer needs and preferences when appropriate.

Memorable service experiences often evoke emotions in customers. Brands can create positive emotional connections by introducing surprise elements into the service journey. These unexpected, delightful moments can leave a lasting impression. Here are some approaches to emotional engagement:

Surprise Gifts or Upgrades: Offer unexpected gifts, discounts, or upgrades as tokens of appreciation for customer loyalty or to celebrate special occasions.

Personalized Thank-You Notes: Include personalized thank-you notes or messages with purchases, deliveries, or service interactions to show genuine appreciation.

Anticipate Customer Needs: Train employees to anticipate customer needs and proactively address them, exceeding expectations in the process.

Create Memorable Moments: Identify opportunities to create

memorable moments, such as celebrating customer milestones or achievements, and make these moments special.

Consistent Follow-Up: Follow up with customers after their interaction to ensure satisfaction and express gratitude for their business.

Technology plays a crucial role in shaping service experiences. By integrating technology effectively, businesses can provide seamless and convenient omnichannel experiences that customers find memorable. Key elements of this strategy include:

User-Friendly Platforms: Ensure that digital platforms, such as websites and mobile apps, are user-friendly, intuitive, and responsive across devices.

Self-Service Options: Offer self-service options that allow customers to access information, make purchases, or resolve issues independently when they choose.

Data Integration: Leverage data from various touchpoints to provide personalized recommendations and anticipate customer needs.

Responsive Customer Support: Implement chatbots, virtual assistants, or live chat options to provide immediate assistance and support on digital platforms.

Feedback Mechanisms: Use technology to gather customer feedback and reviews, which can help improve service quality and identify areas for enhancement.

Creating memorable service experiences is a strategic imperative for businesses looking to build strong customer relationships and foster brand loyalty. These experiences are the result of personalization, exceptional employee training, consistency, emotional engagement, and effective technology integration. By prioritizing these strategies, companies can differentiate themselves in a competitive market, leaving a positive and lasting impression on their customers. Ultimately, a memorable service experience can become a powerful tool for customer retention, advocacy, and sustainable business growth.

The Price of Convenience

In today's fast-paced world, convenience has become a prized commodity. Consumers are increasingly willing to pay a premium for products and services that offer them time-saving, effortless experiences. This phenomenon, known as the psychology of consumers paying more for convenience, is a fascinating aspect of consumer behavior that has significant implications for businesses and marketers. In this exploration, we will delve deep into the underlying psychological factors that drive consumers to make such choices. We will examine the motivations, emotions, and cognitive processes that influence their decisions to prioritize convenience over cost-efficiency.

One of the primary drivers behind consumers paying more for convenience is the value they place on time. Time is an irreplaceable resource, and many consumers are willing to trade money for time-saving solutions. Research in behavioral economics highlights the concept of "time discounting," where individuals place a higher value on immediate rewards compared to future gains. Convenience often offers immediate gratification by reducing the effort and time required for a task. This instant reward triggers a positive emotional response, making consumers more inclined to choose convenient options even if they come at a higher price. For instance, fast food chains charge a premium for ready-made meals, tapping into consumers' desire for quick, hassle-free dining experiences.

Consumers' willingness to pay more for convenience can also be attributed to various cognitive biases that affect decision-making. One such bias is the "anchoring effect," where consumers anchor their decisions based on the first piece of information they receive. When a convenient option is presented first, it establishes a reference point, making it more likely for consumers to choose it, even if it comes at a higher cost. Furthermore, the "status quo bias" leads consumers to stick with familiar and convenient choices, as change requires effort and can be mentally taxing. This bias is evident in subscription-based services where consumers continue paying monthly fees for convenience, even if they no longer use the service regularly.

The psychology of paying more for convenience is not purely rational; it also has a significant emotional component. Convenience often leads to feelings of relief, reduced stress, and enhanced well-being. When consumers experience these positive emotions, they are more likely to justify the higher cost associated with convenience. Moreover, the anticipation of these emotions can be a driving force behind their choices. For example, individuals may choose a more expensive, convenient commuting option because it offers a less stressful daily routine, leading to increased overall life satisfaction. Businesses tap into this emotional aspect by marketing their products and services as time-saving and stress-reducing solutions.

In conclusion, the psychology of consumers paying more for convenience is a multifaceted phenomenon shaped by the interplay of time valuation, cognitive biases, and emotional satisfaction. Understanding these psychological factors is crucial for businesses and marketers seeking to cater to consumer preferences effectively. Offering convenient solutions can create a competitive advantage and allow businesses to command higher prices for their products and services. As consumers continue to lead increasingly busy lives, the demand for convenience is likely to grow, making it essential for businesses to adapt and innovate in response to these evolving consumer behaviors. Ultimately, the willingness to pay more for convenience reflects the intricate balance between financial considerations and the intangible, yet powerful, value of time and emotional well-being in modern society.

The Psychology of Lights and Sounds

Arcade machines and slot machines have long been celebrated for their capacity to captivate and entertain consumers. Beyond their visual aesthetics and gameplay mechanics, both these gaming devices leverage the psychology of lights and sounds to create immersive and compelling experiences. This section embarks on a journey into the intricate world of these sensory stimuli, exploring how the interplay of lights and sounds affects consumer behavior, emotions, and engagement. From the mesmerizing glow of arcade cabinets to the jingling of coins in slot machines, these elements are carefully orchestrated to maximize enjoyment and, in the case of slot machines, potentially influence spending.

The visual impact of lights is a critical component of the psychology of arcade and slot machines. Arcade cabinets, adorned with colorful displays and blinking LEDs, are designed to capture attention and invite players into a world of gaming excitement. Lights not only serve as eye-catching embellishments but also convey essential information, such as game instructions, scores, and power-ups.

In the realm of slot machines, the role of lights is equally significant. The spinning reels, illuminated symbols, and flashing paylines create a dynamic visual spectacle that draws players in. The anticipation of the next spin, accentuated by the vibrant lights, contributes to the thrill of the game. The juxtaposition of vivid colors and patterns can stimulate excitement and curiosity, enticing players to continue spinning the reels.

Sounds in arcade and slot machines serve as auditory cues that enhance the gaming experience. The psychology of sound in these contexts is multifaceted. Sound effects, music, and even the mechanical noises of the machines play essential roles in shaping player emotions and behaviors.

In arcade machines, sound effects contribute to the immersive quality of gameplay. The "ding" of a pinball machine, the explosions in a shoot-'em-up game, or the chirping of a successful character move all create auditory feedback that reinforces player actions. These sounds provide instant gratification and feedback, encouraging players to continue their efforts and potentially spend more time and money.

Slot machines take sound psychology to a new level. The inclusion of music and jingles in slot games enhances the overall ambiance and excitement. Winning combinations trigger celebratory sounds, such as fanfares or jingling coins, creating a positive reinforcement loop. These sounds can elicit feelings of happiness and accomplishment, compelling players to chase the thrill of another win. On the other hand, the suspenseful background music during non-winning spins maintains player engagement and encourages perseverance.

Both lights and sounds in arcade and slot machines are employed as tools of operant conditioning, a psychological concept pioneered by B.F. Skinner. Operant conditioning involves modifying behavior through rewards or punishments. In the context of gaming, this means that players are conditioned to engage with the machines repeatedly in pursuit of rewards and positive feedback.

In arcade games, the immediate visual and auditory feedback after achieving a high score or completing a challenging level reinforces player behavior. The lights and sounds serve as rewards, signaling success and motivating players to continue their quest for more rewards and higher scores.

Slot machines employ a similar principle of operant

conditioning but with a heightened level of unpredictability. The intermittent nature of winning outcomes, accompanied by the sensory delight of lights and sounds, reinforces the behavior of playing and betting. Players experience a rush of excitement during wins, leading to the desire for more wins and the potential for a psychological "near-miss" phenomenon, where players come close to winning but fall just short. This near-miss effect can keep players engaged and willing to continue playing in pursuit of elusive jackpots.

The combination of lights and sounds in slot machines has implications beyond engagement and enjoyment; it can significantly influence consumer spending behavior. The allure of jackpots and the emotional highs generated by winning sounds and lights can lead players to invest more money and time in these machines.

Slot machines are designed with a concept known as "losses disguised as wins" (LDWs). LDWs occur when a player bets and wins an amount that is less than their initial wager. While players perceive these outcomes as wins due to the accompanying celebratory lights and sounds, they are, in reality, losses. This psychological trickery can lead players to underestimate their losses and continue playing, contributing to increased spending.

The hypnotic effect of lights and sounds in slot machines can lead players into a state of "flow," a psychological concept coined by Mihaly Csikszentmihalyi. In this state, individuals become fully absorbed in an activity, losing track of time and external distractions. The captivating lights and sounds of slot machines can induce this flow state, making players more susceptible to continuous play and higher spending.

As we investigate into the psychology of lights and sounds in arcade and slot machines, it is crucial to address the ethical implications of their use. While these sensory elements are integral to the gaming experience, they can also lead to problematic gambling behavior and addiction in vulnerable individuals.

Responsible gaming practices must be implemented to protect consumers from excessive spending and potential harm. This includes providing clear information on odds, implementing spending limits, and offering support for individuals experiencing gambling-related issues. Ethical considerations should always take precedence over profit motives when designing and operating gaming machines.

The psychology of lights and sounds in arcade and slot machines is a multifaceted realm that combines visual and auditory elements to create immersive and engaging experiences. These sensory stimuli serve as powerful tools to capture attention, reinforce player behavior, and influence spending. While they contribute to the excitement and enjoyment of gaming, ethical considerations and responsible gaming practices are essential to ensure that individuals are not negatively impacted by their use. Understanding the intricate interplay of lights and sounds in these gaming contexts is key to crafting consumer experiences that balance entertainment with ethical responsibility.

The Psychology of Warranties and Returns

Warranties and returns are integral components of consumer protection and satisfaction in the modern marketplace. These policies are designed to instill confidence in consumers, assuring them that they are making a wise investment and can rectify any issues that may arise with their purchases. However, the psychology behind warranties and returns goes beyond mere paperwork and policies; it delves into the intricate workings of consumer behavior and decision-making processes. In this section, we will explore the multifaceted aspects of the psychology of warranties and returns, shedding light on how these mechanisms impact consumer choices, perceptions, and overall satisfaction.

Warranties, often presented as a promise of product quality and durability, play a significant role in building trust between consumers and manufacturers or retailers. The psychology behind this trust is rooted in the principle of risk reduction. When consumers see a product backed by a warranty, it reduces their perception of risk associated with the purchase. They believe that if the product fails to meet their expectations or encounters issues, they have a safety net in the form of the warranty to fall back on.

Studies have shown that the presence of a warranty can positively influence purchasing decisions. Consumers are more likely to choose a product with a warranty over one without, even if it comes at a slightly higher price. This behavior is driven by the psychological comfort of knowing that they have a safety net, and it reflects the innate desire to minimize potential regret or loss associated with a purchase.

While warranties provide a sense of security, they can also create what is known as the "illusion of security." This phenomenon occurs when consumers perceive a warranty as a guarantee of flawless performance, leading them to overlook the fine print and assume that any issue will be effortlessly resolved. This perception can have unintended consequences, as consumers may neglect proper product care or usage guidelines, believing that they are protected no matter what.

The psychology of warranties can sometimes lead to a delay in seeking resolution for issues. Consumers may postpone addressing a problem, assuming that it will not worsen or that they can always avail themselves of the warranty later. This delay can result in increased frustration and inconvenience when they finally decide to pursue a return or repair, as the warranty may have expired or its terms changed.

Return policies, on the other hand, are a crucial aspect of post-purchase psychology. They address the fear of buyer's remorse, which is the anxiety and regret consumers feel after making a purchase. An accommodating return policy can significantly alleviate this fear, making consumers more comfortable with their purchase decisions.

Retailers with lenient return policies benefit from a more positive perception in consumers' minds. Customers are more likely to make a purchase if they know they can return it hassle-free if it doesn't meet their expectations. This is particularly important in industries where the product cannot be thoroughly evaluated before purchase, such as online shopping. Consumers rely on the return policy as a safety net, allowing them to experience the product firsthand without the fear of irreversible consequences.

While warranties and return policies are designed to increase consumer satisfaction, they can sometimes lead to a paradoxical effect. Knowing they have the option to return a product may make consumers more critical and less forgiving of minor imperfections or perceived flaws. They may become hyper-aware of any shortcomings, even if they would have overlooked them in the absence of a return policy.

This paradox can put pressure on manufacturers and retailers to meet exceptionally high standards to avoid returns and warranty claims. It underscores the importance of not only offering these policies but also delivering on the quality promised, as failure to do so can result in damaged brand reputation and customer trust.

The psychology of warranties and returns also has a significant emotional dimension. The process of returning a product or making a warranty claim can be emotionally charged for consumers. They may experience frustration, disappointment, or even guilt, depending on the circumstances. On the other hand, a smooth and hassle-free return experience can lead to feelings of relief and satisfaction, enhancing the overall customer relationship.

Manufacturers and retailers can leverage this emotional dimension by ensuring that their customer service teams are well-trained to handle returns and warranty claims empathetically. A positive experience during the resolution process can turn a dissatisfied customer into a loyal one, as they feel their concerns are genuinely acknowledged and addressed.

The psychology of warranties and returns is a complex interplay of trust, risk perception, security, and emotional responses. Understanding these psychological aspects is essential for manufacturers and retailers to create policies and practices that not only protect consumer interests but also enhance their overall satisfaction and loyalty. Warranties and return policies, when strategically implemented and effectively managed, can be powerful tools for building consumer trust, mitigating risk, and ensuring a positive shopping experience in the ever-evolving world of commerce.

The Psychology of Gambling

Gambling is a multifaceted phenomenon that has intrigued, captivated, and challenged individuals for centuries. It is a unique area of consumer behavior, one characterized by both exhilaration and risk. To understand the psychology of gambling for the consumer is to explore into the complex interplay of cognitive processes, emotions, and motivations that drive individuals to participate in games of chance. This section embarks on a comprehensive exploration of the psychology of gambling, dissecting the factors that influence consumer decisions, the allure of risk and reward, and the importance of responsible play.

At the core of gambling's psychology lies the captivating interplay between risk and reward. Humans are inherently drawn to uncertainty and the thrill of unpredictability. The act of placing a bet or buying a lottery ticket is a manifestation of this attraction to risk, as it represents the possibility of winning a prize, often a substantial one.

The anticipation of potential rewards triggers the release of dopamine in the brain, a neurotransmitter associated with pleasure and reinforcement. When individuals gamble, they experience heightened states of excitement and arousal. This emotional rollercoaster, with its peaks of anticipation and valleys of disappointment, contributes to the allure of gambling, making it a unique form of entertainment.

Cognitive biases play a pivotal role in the psychology of gambling. These are systematic patterns of deviation from norm or rationality in judgment, often leading individuals to make irrational decisions. In the context of gambling, several cognitive biases come into play.

The "gambler's fallacy" is one such bias, where individuals believe that past outcomes influence future events in games of chance. For example, if a roulette wheel has landed on red several times in a row, some may believe that black is "due" to come up, despite the odds remaining constant. This fallacy can lead individuals to make irrational bets based on perceived patterns that do not exist.

Another bias is the "illusion of control," which makes people overestimate their ability to influence the outcome of chance-based games. Gamblers may believe that their actions, such as choosing specific numbers in a lottery or rolling dice in a certain way, can impact the results. This belief in control can lead to increased gambling behavior.

For some consumers, gambling serves as a form of escapism from everyday life and its associated stresses. The casino or gambling environment offers a temporary reprieve from personal challenges, providing a space where individuals can immerse themselves in an alternate reality. The allure of this escape, coupled with the anticipation of potential rewards, can be particularly enticing.

Gambling can function as a means of emotional regulation. The highs and lows experienced during gambling can temporarily distract individuals from negative emotions, offering a sense of euphoria during wins and a diversion from life's difficulties. This emotional rollercoaster can be psychologically rewarding, creating a cycle of repeated gambling behavior.

While gambling offers excitement and entertainment for many, it has a dark side that cannot be ignored. Problem gambling and gambling addiction are serious concerns that affect individuals and their families. The psychology of addiction reveals the mechanisms that underlie compulsive gambling.

Individuals with gambling addiction often experience a loss of control over their gambling behavior, with an increasing need to bet larger sums of money to achieve the same level of excitement. This craving for the thrill of gambling can lead to financial, emotional, and social consequences.

The availability of gambling opportunities, particularly in the digital age, exacerbates the risk of addiction. Online gambling platforms offer convenient access to a wide range of games, and the lack of physical presence in a casino can make it easier for individuals to lose track of time and money. Understanding the psychology of addiction is crucial for designing responsible gambling interventions and support systems.

Responsible gambling initiatives aim to promote informed and mindful gambling behavior. Consumers are encouraged to set limits on their gambling activities, both in terms of time and money. Self-exclusion programs, which allow individuals to voluntarily ban themselves from gambling venues, are also part of these initiatives.

Raising awareness about the potential risks of gambling and the signs of problem gambling is vital. It empowers consumers to make informed choices and seek help when needed. Education and access to resources for problem gamblers are essential components of responsible gambling efforts.

The psychology of gambling for the consumer is a fascinating exploration of risk and reward, cognitive biases, emotional regulation, and the challenges of responsible play. Understanding the intricate interplay of these factors is vital for individuals who choose to engage in gambling activities and for society as a whole. While gambling can offer entertainment and excitement, it also carries risks that demand careful consideration. Responsible gambling practices, education, and support systems are essential for promoting healthy and informed consumer choices in the world of gambling.

The Psychology of Nicotine
and the Consumer

Nicotine, a highly addictive compound found in tobacco, has long been a subject of fascination and concern within the realm of consumer psychology. Understanding the intricate psychology of nicotine and how it influences consumer behavior is not only essential for addressing the global health crisis of tobacco addiction but also for comprehending the multifaceted interactions between substance use, marketing, and human psychology. This section embarks into the complex world of nicotine and its impact on consumers, exploring the cognitive and emotional mechanisms that drive tobacco consumption, addiction, and the pursuit of cessation.

Nicotine's allure to consumers begins with the pleasurable sensations it induces. When nicotine is inhaled through smoking or other delivery methods, it binds to nicotinic receptors in the brain, triggering the release of neurotransmitters like dopamine and norepinephrine. These neurotransmitters are associated with feelings of pleasure, reward, and alertness. Consequently, nicotine provides an immediate sense of euphoria and heightened alertness, creating a reinforcing loop that encourages continued use.

This pleasurable experience is a fundamental component of the psychology of nicotine. The brain learns to associate the act of smoking or using nicotine products with pleasure, leading consumers to seek out nicotine to replicate those positive sensations. Over time, this association becomes deeply ingrained, contributing to the development of addiction.

Nicotine consumption often becomes intertwined with habit and ritual, further complicating the psychology of tobacco addiction. For many smokers, cigarettes become associated with specific daily routines or situations, such as having a smoke with morning coffee or during social gatherings. These rituals provide a sense of comfort and familiarity, making it challenging to break the habit.

The role of habit and ritual in nicotine use underscores the psychological dimensions of addiction. It's not just the physiological craving for nicotine that drives continued use; it's also the psychological dependence on the associated rituals and routines. Understanding and addressing these psychological triggers is crucial for individuals attempting to quit smoking.

The psychology of nicotine is profoundly influenced by advertising and marketing strategies employed by tobacco companies. For decades, the tobacco industry has invested vast sums in promoting their products through clever marketing campaigns that tap into consumers' desires for social acceptance, independence, and glamour. Iconic figures like the Marlboro Man and slogans like "You've come a long way, baby" have become embedded in the collective psyche.

Marketing plays a significant role in shaping consumer perceptions of nicotine products. The allure of rebellion, sophistication, or belonging to a particular group can be powerful motivators for trying and continuing to use tobacco. Understanding the psychological tactics used by the tobacco industry is essential for public health efforts to counteract the appeal of smoking.

Nicotine addiction is characterized by a vicious cycle that perpetuates continued use. As individuals develop a tolerance to nicotine, they require increasing amounts to achieve the desired effects. This escalation in consumption deepens physical dependence, making quitting even more challenging. Additionally, the withdrawal symptoms that occur when nicotine levels drop—such as irritability, anxiety, and difficulty concentrating—create powerful incentives to maintain nicotine intake.

The psychology of nicotine addiction is marked by an ongoing internal struggle. Smokers often find themselves caught between the desire to quit for health reasons and the powerful psychological and physical forces that keep them smoking. This internal conflict can contribute to feelings of guilt, shame, and low self-esteem, further complicating cessation efforts.

Despite the formidable challenges of nicotine addiction, many consumers seek ways to quit smoking or using tobacco products. The psychology of cessation involves understanding the factors that drive individuals to make this critical decision and the behavioral interventions that can support their efforts.

Behavioral interventions, such as counseling and cognitive-behavioral therapy, are based on principles of operant conditioning and learning theory. These approaches help individuals identify triggers for smoking, develop coping strategies, and rewire the associations between nicotine use and pleasure. Behavioral interventions recognize that nicotine addiction is not solely a matter of physiological dependence but also a complex interplay of habits, rituals, and psychological factors.

The psychology of nicotine and the consumer is a multifaceted domain that encompasses pleasure, habit, marketing influence, addiction, and the pursuit of cessation. Understanding these intricate psychological dynamics is essential for addressing the global health challenge of tobacco addiction. It highlights the need for comprehensive strategies that combine physiological and psychological approaches to help individuals overcome nicotine dependence and make informed choices about their health. Additionally, efforts to regulate and counteract tobacco marketing and advertising play a pivotal role in preventing the initiation of nicotine use and curbing the tobacco epidemic.

Ultimately, unraveling the psychology of nicotine offers insights into the complex interplay of human behavior, addiction, and public health.

The Future of Consumer Psychology

Consumer psychology, the study of how individuals make decisions and interact with products, services, and brands, is a dynamic field that continues to evolve rapidly. As we step into an era defined by digital transformation, evolving consumer expectations, and ethical considerations, the future of consumer psychology presents both exciting opportunities and complex challenges. This section explores five key themes that offer insights into the future of consumer psychology: the impact of emerging technologies, the shift towards conscious consumerism, the personalization paradox, the importance of trust and ethics, and the role of data and analytics.

The future of consumer psychology is intricately tied to emerging technologies that are reshaping how consumers interact with businesses. Augmented reality (AR), virtual reality (VR), artificial intelligence (AI), and the Internet of Things (IoT) are becoming integral parts of the consumer experience. AR and VR, for instance, are poised to revolutionize shopping by allowing consumers to virtually try on products or experience them in immersive environments. AI-powered chatbots and personalized recommendation engines are enhancing customer service and product discovery. The IoT connects everyday objects to the internet, creating opportunities for smart homes and personalized experiences.

The integration of these technologies also raises questions about data privacy, security, and the potential for manipulation. Consumer psychologists will need to explore how these technologies affect consumer decision-making, trust, and well-being while navigating the ethical implications associated with their use.

A significant shift is underway towards conscious consumerism, where consumers prioritize values, sustainability, and ethical considerations in their purchasing decisions. This shift reflects a growing awareness of environmental and social issues, as well as a desire for transparency from brands. Consumer psychologists will play a pivotal role in understanding how these values influence consumer choices and how businesses can authentically align with them.

Brands that embrace sustainability, ethical sourcing, and social responsibility are likely to resonate more with conscious consumers. However, the challenge lies in effectively communicating these efforts without being seen as engaging in "greenwashing" or merely paying lip service to important issues. The future of consumer psychology will involve studying the motivations and behaviors of conscious consumers and helping brands navigate this evolving landscape.

As businesses collect vast amounts of data on consumer preferences and behaviors, personalization has become a cornerstone of marketing strategies. Personalized product recommendations, tailored content, and customized experiences have the potential to enhance consumer satisfaction and drive sales. However, there is a fine line between personalization and invasion of privacy.

Consumer psychologists will need to explore the personalization paradox—the tension between delivering tailored experiences and respecting individual privacy. Striking the right balance is critical to maintaining consumer trust. Ethical considerations, data protection regulations, and consumer consent will shape the future of personalization strategies.

Trust is at the heart of the consumer-brand relationship, and consumer psychologists will increasingly focus on understanding the factors that influence trust in a digital age. Trustworthiness is closely linked to transparency, data security, ethical practices, and consistent brand messaging.

Ethical considerations in consumer psychology encompass not only data privacy but also issues like behavioral nudging, persuasive design techniques, and the responsible use of AI. Researchers in the field will explore how businesses can build and maintain trust by adopting ethical practices and communicating them effectively to consumers.

Data and analytics are revolutionizing consumer psychology, providing insights into consumer behavior at an unprecedented level of granularity. Advanced analytics, including machine learning and predictive modeling, enable businesses to anticipate consumer preferences and trends. This data-driven approach allows for more effective marketing campaigns, improved product design, and enhanced customer experiences.

The sheer volume of data and the need for sophisticated analytics raise questions about data security, bias in algorithms, and the ethical use of consumer information. Consumer psychologists will need to collaborate with data scientists and ethicists to address these challenges and ensure that data-driven insights benefit both businesses and consumers.

The future of consumer psychology is a complex and ever-evolving landscape, shaped by emerging technologies, shifting consumer values, the personalization paradox, the importance of trust and ethics, and the role of data and analytics. Consumer psychologists will play a crucial role in understanding and navigating these dynamics, helping businesses create meaningful and ethical consumer experiences in an increasingly digital and interconnected world. As the field continues to evolve, its insights will be invaluable for businesses seeking to connect with consumers in more authentic, responsible, and effective ways.

Consumer behavior is a dynamic field that continuously evolves in response to changing societal, technological, and economic factors. Staying attuned to emerging trends in consumer behavior is essential for businesses seeking to adapt, innovate, and meet the evolving demands and expectations of their customers. We will explore five significant emerging trends in consumer behavior: the rise of conscious consumerism, the impact of digital transformation, the importance of social media influence, the growth of online marketplaces, and the pursuit of experiential shopping.

One of the most prominent emerging trends in consumer behavior is the rise of conscious consumerism. Today's consumers are increasingly focused on making ethical, sustainable, and socially responsible choices in their purchasing decisions. They seek products and brands that align with their values, whether it's supporting eco-friendly practices, fair labor conditions, or charitable causes.

This trend reflects a growing awareness of environmental and social issues, as well as a desire for transparency and authenticity from brands. Consumers want to know the story behind the products they buy and are willing to pay a premium for items that reflect their values. Brands that embrace sustainability, ethical sourcing, and social responsibility are likely to resonate more with conscious consumers. Understanding and catering to this trend is crucial for businesses aiming to build trust and loyalty with this discerning consumer segment.

Digital transformation has had a profound impact on consumer behavior. The ubiquity of smartphones, the growth of e-commerce, and the rise of digital payment options have reshaped how consumers research, shop, and interact with brands. Online shopping offers convenience, a vast product selection, and personalized recommendations, all of which have become integral to the modern consumer experience.

The COVID-19 pandemic accelerated the adoption of digital

shopping, as lockdowns and safety concerns prompted consumers to shift their preferences toward online channels. Even as the pandemic recedes, the digital-first habits formed during this period are likely to persist.

Businesses must adapt to these changes by optimizing their online presence, improving the user experience, and leveraging data and analytics to better understand and meet the needs of digital consumers. The integration of augmented reality (AR) and virtual reality (VR) technologies into online shopping experiences is also on the horizon, offering new opportunities for engagement and personalization.

Social media platforms have become influential sources of product discovery and brand engagement, making the role of social media influence a significant trend in consumer behavior. Consumers turn to platforms like Instagram, TikTok, and YouTube for inspiration, product reviews, and recommendations from influencers and peers.

The impact of social media on consumer behavior extends beyond awareness; it also plays a critical role in shaping purchasing decisions. Consumers trust recommendations from people they follow and relate to, even if those individuals are not traditional celebrities. The authenticity and relatability of influencers can sway consumer choices, especially among younger demographics.

Brands are increasingly leveraging influencer marketing strategies to connect with consumers authentically. The challenge lies in finding the right influencers whose values align with the brand and resonate with the target audience. Understanding the dynamics of social media influence is essential for businesses aiming to harness its power effectively.

Online marketplaces, such as Amazon, eBay, and Alibaba, have experienced explosive growth and are reshaping consumer behavior. These platforms offer a wide range of products, competitive pricing, and convenient one-stop shopping experiences. Consumers appreciate the convenience of browsing multiple sellers, reading reviews, and comparing prices within a single marketplace.

Online marketplaces have also empowered small businesses and independent sellers to reach a global audience, leveling the playing field with established brands. As a result, consumers have access to a more diverse and unique range of products than ever before.

This trend has implications for both consumers and businesses. Consumers benefit from increased choices and competitive pricing, but they must also navigate issues like counterfeit products and data privacy concerns. Businesses must adapt by considering the role of online marketplaces in their distribution strategies and exploring opportunities for collaboration or direct-to-consumer sales.

Amidst the convenience of online shopping, there is a growing desire among consumers for experiential shopping. Consumers seek memorable and immersive in-store experiences that go beyond mere transactions. They want to engage with brands, participate in interactive demonstrations, and enjoy memorable moments while shopping.

Retailers are responding to this trend by investing in experiential retail spaces. Brick-and-mortar stores are designed as destinations where consumers can explore, learn, and engage with products and brands. For example, some fashion retailers are incorporating augmented reality mirrors that allow customers to virtually try on clothing, while others offer interactive workshops or in-store events.

Experiential shopping recognizes that the physical store can provide something unique that online channels cannot—a multisensory and tactile experience. This trend underscores the importance of creating environments that resonate with consumers on an emotional and personal level.

Emerging trends in consumer behavior are reshaping the way businesses engage with their customers. The rise of conscious consumerism, the impact of digital transformation, the importance of social media influence, the growth of online marketplaces, and the pursuit of experiential shopping experiences are all influencing consumer choices and expectations. To remain competitive and meet the evolving demands of consumers, businesses must adapt, innovate, and prioritize strategies that align with these trends. Understanding the psychology behind these trends is essential for building strong customer relationships, enhancing brand loyalty, and driving success in a rapidly changing marketplace.

Conclusion

In "Understanding the Minds of Buyers," we embarked on a captivating journey through the intricate landscape of consumer psychology, decoding the thought processes, emotions, and behaviors that drive purchasing decisions. Throughout this exploration, we've delved deep into the minds of buyers, unraveling the complex interplay of factors that influence how and why consumers make choices. As we conclude this enlightening journey, it is evident that grasping the dynamics of consumer psychology is not just a scholarly pursuit; it's a vital skill for individuals and businesses seeking to thrive in an ever-evolving marketplace.

Our voyage commenced with the recognition that consumer psychology is a multifaceted discipline that extends far beyond superficial observations of buying behavior. By peering into the minds of buyers, we unearthed profound insights into the drivers of consumer choices. From the influence of emotions to the significance of social and cultural factors, understanding the intricate web of forces that shape consumers' decisions empowers us to anticipate, connect, and engage with them on a deeper level.

As we ventured deeper into the realm of consumer psychology, we uncovered the art and science of persuasion. We unveiled the psychology of influence, exploring techniques such as reciprocity, scarcity, authority, and social proof that marketers and salespeople employ to sway consumer decisions. Recognizing the persuasive power of these principles equips us with the tools to ethically and effectively communicate our offerings and ideas in a crowded marketplace.

Our journey evolved to encompass the digital landscape, where technology and online platforms have revolutionized how buyers engage with brands. We dissected the impact of digital transformation on consumer behavior, from the convenience of e-commerce to the rise of social media influence. In this digital era, understanding the minds of buyers means adapting to their changing preferences, harnessing the power of data-driven insights, and leveraging technology to create meaningful and personalized interactions.

Consumer psychology isn't solely about persuading buyers; it also carries a profound ethical imperative. We explored the ethical considerations inherent in consumer behavior, from issues of privacy and data protection to the rise of conscious consumerism. The modern consumer is more discerning, values-driven, and socially conscious than ever before. Embracing ethics in marketing and business practices is not just a moral obligation but also a strategic imperative for long-term success.

As we conclude our journey, we stand at the cusp of an exciting and uncertain future in the world of consumer psychology. Emerging trends, such as conscious consumerism, the impact of artificial intelligence, and the pursuit of experiential shopping, present both opportunities and challenges. However, what remains steadfast is the enduring importance of understanding the minds of buyers. In the age of constant change, the ability to empathize, connect, and adapt to the evolving needs and desires of consumers will be the North Star guiding businesses to prosperity.

In the pages of "Understanding the Minds of Buyers," we have explored the intricate tapestry of consumer psychology, uncovering the threads that weave together emotions, rationality, and cultural influences in the purchase decision-making process. We've examined the tactics that persuade and the ethical principles that guide. We've navigated the digital landscape and contemplated the ethical responsibilities that come with the power to influence.

This book has been a journey of discovery, a testament to the ever-evolving nature of consumer behavior, and a reminder of the importance of embracing change, ethics, and empathy in our interactions with buyers. As we part ways, let us carry forth the wisdom gained here, armed with a deeper understanding of the minds of buyers, ready to navigate the shifting tides of consumer psychology, and to thrive in an exciting and dynamic marketplace where connection, trust, and authenticity are the keys to success.